C000244642

THE ROYAL COURT THEATRE PRESENTS

Scenes with girls

by Miriam Battye

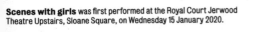

Scenes with girls was first performed at the Royal Court Jerwood
Theatre Upstairs, Sloane Square, on Wednesday 15 January 2020.

Scenes with girls
by Miriam Battye

CAST (in alphabetical order)

Lou **Rebekah Murrell**
Tosh **Tanya Reynolds**
Fran **Letty Thomas**

Director **Lucy Morrison**
Designer **Naomi Dawson**
Lighting Designer **Nao Nagai**
Sound Designer **Beth Duke**
Movement Director **Delphine Gaborit**
Assistant Director **TD. Moyo**
Casting Director **Amy Ball**
Production Manager **Simon Evans**
Costume Supervisor **Katie Price**
Stage Managers **Katie Bachtler, Julia Slienger**
Set built by **Royal Court Stage Department**

Scenes with girls
by Miriam Battye

Miriam Battye (Writer)

Theatre includes: **Trip the Light Fantastic (Bristol Old Vic); All Your Gold (Theatre Royal, Plymouth); Electricity (NYT/Arcola); Balance (Royal Exchange, Manchester); Pancake Day (Bunker/PLAY).**

Miriam was the first Sister Pictures Writer in Residence in 2018 and has various original ideas in development for television.

Naomi Dawson (Designer)

For the Royal Court: **The Woods, Men in the Cities (& Traverse/UK tour).**

Other theatre includes: **Light Falls, Happy Days (Royal Exchange, Manchester); The Convert, The Container, Phaedra's Love, The Pope's Wedding, Forest of Thorns (Young Vic); As You Like It (Regent's Park Open Air); The Duchess of Malfi, Doctor Faustus, The White Devil, The Roaring Girl, As You Like It, King John (RSC); The Winter's Tale (Romateatern, Gotland); The Tin Drum (Kneehigh/Liverpool Everyman/Leeds Playhouse); Beryl (Leeds Playhouse/UK tour); Much Ado About Nothing (Rose, Kingston); Kasimir & Karoline, Fanny & Alexander, Love & Money (Malmö Stadsteater, Sweden); Mirabel (Ovalhouse); Every One (BAC); Weaklings (Warwick Arts Centre); Hotel, Three More Sleepless Nights (National); Wildefire, Belongings, The Gods Weep (Hampstead); Brave New World, Dancing at Lughnasa, In Praise of Love (Royal & Derngate, Northampton); Monkey Bars (Unicorn/Traverse); Landscape & Monologue (Ustinov, Bath); Amerika, Krieg der Bilder (Staatstheater Mainz, Germany); Scorched (Old Vic Tunnels); Mary Shelley, The Glass Menagerie, Speechless (Shared Experience); The Typist (Sky Arts); King Pelican, Speed Death of the Radiant Child (Drum, Plymouth); If That's All There Is (Lyric, Hammersmith); ...Sisters (& Headlong), State of Emergency, Mariana Pineda (Gate); Stallerhof, Richard III, The Cherry Orchard, Summer Begins (Southwark); Attempts on Her Life, Widows, Touched (BAC); Home, In Blood, Venezuela, Mud, Trash (Arcola).**

Opera includes: **Madama Butterfly, The Lottery, The Fairy Queen (Bury Court Opera); Madama Butterfly (Arcola).**

Beth Duke (Sound Designer)

As sound designer, theatre includes: **One Under (Graeae/UK tour); Superstar (& Southwark), Fox (Edinburgh Festival Fringe); Together, Not the Same (Sadler's Wells); New Views (National); Queen Margaret, 5, 11, Emilia (Mountview); Great Expectations (Geffrye Museum); Lovely & Jason, Boots, Split (VAULT Festival); Silence (Mercury/UK tour); Around the Block (Etcetera); Eros (White Bear); Breathe (Tristan Bates); A Fantastic Bohemian, Lovesick (Arcola); Boxman (UK tour); Little Did I Know (Bread & Roses); The State of Things (Brockley Jack Studio).**

As associate sound designer, theatre includes: **War of the Worlds Immersive Experience (56 Leadenhall Street); A Midsummer Night's Dream (Tobacco Factory); Goodbear, Do Our Best (Edinburgh Festival Fringe); Dust (NYTW).**

Film includes: **Gaixia [as sound recordist], Hydrangea [as composer].**

Delphine Gaborit (Movement Director)

For the Royal Court: **seven methods of killing kylie jenner.**

Other theatre includes: **The Suicide (National); Way Up Stream (Chichester Festival).**

As associate movement director, theatre includes: **Pinocchio (National); The Curious Incident of the Dog in the Night-Time (National & International tours); Harry Potter and the Cursed Child (West End).**

As movement coach, film includes: **First Song (short), Wild Rose, Tell It to the Bees, The Titan.**

Delphine trained as a dancer and has been working as a performer for 20 years with choreographers in the UK and across Europe. In 2009 she started a nine year collaboration with Sasha Waltz and Guests in Berlin, joining the company for seven creations touring all over the world. As a movement director, Delphine has worked across theatre, film and visual art. She has collaborated and toured with artists such as Martin Creed for Ballet 1020, Anthea Hamilton for The Squash, her Duveen Galleries commission at Tate Britain, and Adam Linder for his choreographic services.

Lucy Morrison (Director)

For the Royal Court: **The Woods, Lights Out/ It's All Made Up/The Space Between (The Site Programme), MANWATCHING, Plaques & Tangles, Who Cares, Pests, Product (& Clean Break/Traverse/European tour).**

Other theatre includes: **Elephant (Birmingham Rep); Billy the Girl, This Wide Night (Clean Break/Soho); Little on the Inside (Clean Break/ Almeida/Latitude Festival); it felt empty when the heart went at first but it is alright now (Clean Break/Arcola); Fatal Light, Doris Day (Soho).**

Lucy is an Associate Director at the Royal Court.

TD. Moyo (Assistant Director)

As director, theatre includes: **Caste-ing (Nouveau Riche/Barbican); Dark & Lovely (Rose, Kingston); 32 Peak St. (Tristan Bates); Fifty Years (Theatre Royal, Stratford East); Mind Body & Soul (Bussey Building); Dolla (Aphra Studio, University of Kent).**

As writer & director, theatre includes: **FEELS (Lyric, Hammersmith); Jungle [& producer] (Courtyard); Scene (UK tour).**

As resident director, theatre includes: **The Doctor (Almeida/Tour).**

As assistant director, theatre includes: **The Diary of Anne Frank (Headlong); Lovebirds (Aphra Studio, University of Kent).**

TD. is currently Resident Director at The Almeida.

Rebekah Murrell (Lou)

As performer, for the Royal Court: **Glass. Kill. Bluebeard. Imp.**

As performer, other theatre includes: **Whitewash (Soho); Nine Night (National/West End); The Host (Yard).**

As director, theatre includes: **J'Ouvert (Theatre503); Interrupted (JW3).**

As performer, television includes: **Being Victor, Myths, The Roman Mysteries.**

As performer, radio includes: **Blend, The Gift.**

Nao Nagai (Lighting Designer)

Theatre includes: **Yellowman (Young Vic); Putting Words in Your Mouth (Roundhouse); Philip Pullman's Grimm's Tale (Unicorn); Flight Paths (Extant/Yellow Earth/UK tour); Gaping Hole (Ovalhouse); An Anatomy Act (Live Collision!/Athletes of the Heart); Dr Carnesky's Incredible Bleeding Woman (Carnesky Production/International tour); Prurience (Southbank); Fake It Till You Make It (Bryony Kimmings/International tour); DIY Nativity (Cambridge Junction); Copyright Christmas, Ceremonial Blue (Barbican); Familiar (Fierce/ UK tour); The moment I saw you I knew I could love you (curious international/International tour); Restoration of Nell Gwyn, MARIE (Theatre Royal, York/International tour); Ay Carmela!, The Greatest Drummer in the World, The Portraits in Song (Ensemble/International tour); The Great Escape – The Borrowers' Tale (BAC/Kazuko Hohki/International tour); Kwaidan, Urashima (Rouge 28).**

Dance includes: **Night Clubbing, OUT (Rachael Young/International tour); Orchard (Elinor Lewis/International tour); ABOUT US (Jacky Lansley/UK tour).**

Opera includes: **...Madama Butterfly, Rigoletto (& Bury Court Opera), Tosca, The Crane (Arcola); Weather Man (Opera North).**

Tanya Reynolds (Tosh)

Television includes: **Sex Education, Delicious, The Bisexual, Outlander, Rellik.**

Film includes: **Emma, Fanny Lye Deliver'd.**

Scenes with girls is Tanya's professional theatre debut.

Letty Thomas (Fran)

Theatre includes: **The Divide (Old Vic); Mary Stuart (Almeida); Men (Arcola).**

Television includes: **The Crown, For Life, Doc Martin.**

Film includes: **Emma, Uneatable [short].**

THE ROYAL COURT THEATRE

The Royal Court Theatre is the writers' theatre. It is a leading force in world theatre for cultivating and supporting writers – undiscovered, emerging and established.

Through the writers, the Royal Court is at the forefront of creating restless, alert, provocative theatre about now. We open our doors to the unheard voices and free thinkers that, through their writing, change our way of seeing.

Over 120,000 people visit the Royal Court in Sloane Square, London, each year and many thousands more see our work elsewhere through transfers to the West End and New York, UK and international tours, digital platforms, our residencies across London, and our site-specific work. Through all our work we strive to inspire audiences and influence future writers with radical thinking and provocative discussion.

The Royal Court's extensive development activity encompasses a diverse range of writers and artists and includes an ongoing programme of writers' attachments, readings, workshops and playwriting groups. Twenty years of the International Department's pioneering work around the world means the Royal Court has relationships with writers on every continent.

Within the past sixty years, John Osborne, Samuel Beckett, Arnold Wesker, Ann Jellicoe, Howard Brenton and David Hare have started their careers at the Court. Many others including Caryl Churchill, Athol Fugard, Mark Ravenhill, Simon Stephens, debbie tucker green, Sarah Kane – and, more recently, Lucy Kirkwood, Nick Payne, Penelope Skinner and Alistair McDowall – have followed.

The Royal Court has produced many iconic plays from Lucy Kirkwood's **The Children** to Jez Butterworth's **Jerusalem** and Martin McDonagh's **Hangmen**.

Royal Court plays from every decade are now performed on stage and taught in classrooms and universities across the globe.

It is because of this commitment to the writer that we believe there is no more important theatre in the world than the Royal Court.

 royalcourt ◼ royalcourttheatre

Supported using public funding by **ARTS COUNCIL ENGLAND**

ROYAL

COMING UP AT THE ROYAL COURT

15 Jan – 22 Feb

Scenes with girls
By Miriam Battye

30 Jan – 22 Feb

Poet in da Corner
**By Debris Stevenson
(feat. Jammz)**
Originally co-commissioned by 14-18 NOW and the Royal
Court Theatre in 2018, supported by Jerwood Arts

7 Feb – 15 Feb

all of it
By Alistair McDowall

4 – 21 Mar

Shoe Lady
By E.V. Crowe

2 – 25 Apr

Rare Earth Mettle
By Al Smith
Generously supported with a lead gift from Charles
Holloway. Recipient of an Edgerton Foundation New
Play Award. Supported by Cockayne Grant for the
Arts, a donor advised fund of The London
Community Foundation.

9 Apr – 9 May

two Palestinians go dogging
By Sami Ibrahim
Royal Court Theatre and Theatre Uncut

7 – 16 May

The Song Project
**Concept by Chloe Lamford
and Wende**

**Created by Chloe Lamford,
Wende, Isobel Waller-Bridge
and Imogen Knight**

**With words by E.V. Crowe,
Sabrina Mahfouz, Somalia
Seaton, Stef Smith and Debris
Stevenson**

20 May – 20 Jun

A Fight Against...
By Pablo Manzi
Translated by William Gregory
Royal Court Theatre and Teatro a Mil Foundation

royalcourttheatre.com

Sloane Square London, SW1W 8AS
⊖ Sloane Square ⇌ Victoria Station
🐦 royalcourt 📘 theroyalcourttheatre 📷 royalcourttheatre

The London Community Foundation

COCKAYNE

ARTS COUNCIL
ENGLAND
Supported using public funding by

JERWOOD
ARTS

COURT

ASSISTED PERFORMANCES

Captioned Performances

Captioned performances are accessible for D/deaf, deafened & hard of hearing people as well as being suitable for people for whom English is not a first language. There are regular captioned performances in the Jerwood Theatre Downstairs on Wednesdays and the Jerwood Theatre Upstairs on Fridays.

In the Jerwood Theatre Downstairs
Poet in da Corner: Wed 12 & 19 Feb, 7.30pm
all of it: Wed 12 Feb, 9.30pm
Shoe Lady: Wed 18 Mar, 7.30pm
Rare Earth Mettle: Wed 22 Apr, 7.30pm
The Glow: Wed 17, 24 Jun & 1 July, 7.30pm
Is God Is: Wed 5 & 12 Aug, 7.30pm

In the Jerwood Theatre Upstairs
Scenes with girls: Fri 31 Jan, 7, 14 & 21 Feb, 7.45pm
two Palestinians go dogging: Fri 24 Apr, 1 & 8 May, 7.45pm
A Fight Against...: Fri 5, 12 & 19 Jun, 7.45pm

Audio Described Performances

Audio described performances are accessible for blind or partially sighted customers. They are preceded by a touch tour (at 1pm) which allows patrons access to elements of theatre design including set and costume.

In the Jerwood Theatre Downstairs
Shoe Lady: Sat 21 Mar, 2.30pm
Rare Earth Mettle: Sat 25 Apr, 2.30pm
The Glow: Sat 27 Jun, 2.30pm
Is God Is: Sat 8 Aug, 2.30pm

There will be a touch tour (at 1pm) and enhanced pre-show notes for
Poet in da Corner on Sat 22 Feb, 2.30pm

ROYAL

ASSISTED PERFORMANCES

Performances in a Relaxed Environment

Relaxed Environment performances are suitable for those who may benefit from a more relaxed experience.

During these performances:
- There will be a relaxed attitude to noise in the auditorium; you are welcome to respond to the show in whatever way feels natural
- You can enter and exit the auditorium when needed
- We will help you find the best seats
- House lights remained raised slightly
- Loud noises may be reduced

In the Jerwood Theatre Downstairs
Poet in da Corner: Sat 8 Feb, 2.30pm
Rare Earth Mettle: Sat 18 Apr, 2.30pm
The Glow: Sat 13 Jun, 2.30pm
Is God Is: Sat 1 Aug, 2.30pm

In the Jerwood Theatre Upstairs
Scenes with girls: Sat 15 Feb, 3pm
two Palestinians go dogging: Sat 2 May, 3pm
A Fight Against...: Sat 20 Jun, 3pm

If you would like to talk to us about your access requirements please contact our Box Office at (0)20 7565 5000 or **boxoffice@royalcourttheatre.com**
The Royal Court Visual Story is available on our website. We also produce Story Synopsis and Sensory Synopsis which are available on request.

For more information and to book access tickets online, visit

royalcourttheatre.com/access

Sloane Square London, SW1W 8AS ⊖ Sloane Square ⇄ Victoria Station
🐦 royalcourt f theroyalcourttheatre 📷 royalcourttheatre

COURT

ROYAL COURT SUPPORTERS

The Royal Court is a registered charity and not-for-profit company. We need to raise £1.5 million every year in addition to our core grant from the Arts Council and our ticket income to achieve what we do.

We have significant and longstanding relationships with many generous organisations and individuals who provide vital support. Royal Court supporters enable us to remain the writers' theatre, find stories from everywhere and create theatre for everyone.

We can't do it without you.

PUBLIC FUNDING

Arts Council England, London
British Council

TRUSTS & FOUNDATIONS

The Derrill Allatt Foundation
The Backstage Trust
The Austin & Hope Pilkington Trust
The Boshier-Hinton Foundation
Martin Bowley Charitable Trust
The Chapman Charitable Trust
CHK Foundation
The City Bridge Trust
The Cleopatra Trust
Cockayne - Grants for the Arts
The Ernest Cook Trust
The Nöel Coward Foundation
Cowley Charitable Trust
Edgerton Foundation
The Eranda Rothschild Foundation
Lady Antonia Fraser for The Pinter Commission
The Golden Bottle Trust
The Haberdashers' Company
The Paul Hamlyn Foundation
Roderick & Elizabeth Jack
Jerwood Arts
The Leche Trust
The Andrew Lloyd Webber Foundation
The London Community Foundation
John Lyon's Charity
Clare McIntyre's Bursary
Old Possum's Practical Trust
The David & Elaine Potter Foundation
The Richard Radcliffe Charitable Trust
Rose Foundation
Royal Victoria Hall Foundation
The Sobell Foundation
Span Trust
John Thaw Foundation
The Garfield Weston Foundation

CORPORATE SPONSORS

Aqua Financial Limited
Cadogan
Colbert
Edwardian Hotels, London
Fever-Tree
Gedye & Sons
Green Rooms
Greene King
Kirkland & Ellis International LLP
Kudos
MAC

CORPORATE MEMBERS

Platinum
Auriens
Lombard Odier

Gold
Weil, Gotshal & Manges LLP

Silver
Azteca Latin Lounge
Bloomberg
Kekst CNC
Left Bank Pictures
The No 8 Partnership Dental Practice
PATRIZIA
Royal Bank of Canada - Global Asset Management
Tetragon Financial Group

COMMISSION PARTNERS
Oberon Books

For more information or to become a foundation or business supporter contact: support@royalcourttheatre.com/020 7565 5064.

Supported using public funding by
ARTS COUNCIL ENGLAND

ROYAL

BAR & KITCHEN

The Royal Court's Bar & Kitchen aims to create a welcoming and inspiring environment with a style and ethos that reflects the work we put on stage. Our menu consists of simple, ingredient driven and flavour-focused dishes with an emphasis on freshness and seasonality. This is supported by a carefully curated drinks list notable for its excellent wine selection, craft beers and skilfully prepared coffee. By day a perfect spot for long lunches, meetings or quiet reflection and by night an atmospheric, vibrant meeting space for cast, crew, audiences and the general public.

GENERAL OPENING HOURS
Monday – Friday: 10am – late
Saturday: 11am – late

Advance booking is suggested at peak times.

For more information, visit
royalcourttheatre.com/bar

HIRES & EVENTS

The Royal Court is available to hire for celebrations, rehearsals, meetings, filming, ceremonies and much more. Our two theatre spaces can be hired for conferences and showcases, and the building is a unique venue for bespoke weddings and receptions.

For more information, visit
royalcourttheatre.com/events

Sloane Square London, SW1W 8AS ⊖ Sloane Square ⇌ Victoria Station
🐦 royalcourt 🅵 theroyalcourttheatre 📷 royalcourttheatre

COURT

"There are no spaces, no rooms in my opinion, with a greater legacy of fearlessness, truth and clarity than this space."
Simon Stephens, Playwright

The Royal Court invests in the future of the theatre, offering writers the support, time and resources to find their voices and tell their stories, asking the big questions and responding to the issues of the moment.

As a registered charity, the Royal Court needs to raise at least £1.5 million every year in addition to our Arts Council funding and ticket income, to keep seeking out, developing and nurturing new voices. Please join us by donating today.

You can donate online at **royalcourttheatre.com/donate** or via our **donation box in the Bar & Kitchen.**

We can't do it without you.

Support the Court

To find out more about the different ways in which you can be involved please contact support@royalcourttheatre.com/ 020 7565 5049

The English Stage Company at the Royal Court Theatre is a registered charity (No. 231242).

Scenes with girls

Miriam Battye is a writer from Manchester. Her plays includes *Trip the Light Fantastic* (Bristol Old Vic), *All Your Gold* (Theatre Royal, Plymouth), *Electricity* (NYT/Arcola), *Balance* (Royal Exchange, Manchester) and *Pancake Day* (Bunker/PLAY). Miriam was the 2018 Sister Pictures Writer in Residence.

MIRIAM BATTYE

Scenes with girls

FABER & FABER

First published in 2020
by Faber and Faber Limited
74–77 Great Russell Street
London WC1B 3DA

Typeset by JG
Printed and bound in the UK by CPI Group (Ltd), Croydon CR0 4YY

A CIP record for this book
is available from the British Library

978–0–571–35845–8

2 4 6 8 10 9 7 5 3 1

Scenes with girls premiered at the Royal Court Jerwood Theatre Upstairs, London, on 15 January 2020. The cast was as follows:

Lou Rebekah Murrell
Tosh Tanya Reynolds
Fran Letty Thomas

Director Lucy Morrison
Designer Naomi Dawson
Lighting Designer Nao Nagai
Sound Designer Beth Duke
Movement Director Delphine Gaborit
Assistant Director TD Moyo

Acknowledgements

I have many to thank for the fact this play exists now in your hand. Many people took a punt on this weird play and this weird playwright.

First thanks must go to Alice Birch, who led the writers group where this play began, and who encouraged me to write with freedom and without apology. Thank you to that inspiring group of playwrights. To Louise Stephens for inviting me in. Thank you to the Court for paying for my travel to London so I could take part, and thank you for not underestimating how important that was.

Endless thanks to everyone at the Royal Court, to Vicky and her team for commissioning this play, giving me the time and space to keep rewriting. To Ellie, Jane, Amy and Arthur, to everyone upstairs, stage door and front of house.

Thank you to every at Faber & Faber, particularly to Steve King who championed the play and to Jodi Gray who brought it to the page.

Thank you Alex Rusher for being the most incredible agent and friend to me.

Thank you to those who have championed my writing over the years: Sharon Clark, Nick Leather, Jo Coombes, Suzanne Bell, Sam Pritchard, Nik Partridge, Theatre West, Becky Prestwich, Rebecca Durbin, Kat Drury, Matt Harrison, Alice Tyler and Jamie Jackson. And to the actors who lent their talents to early developments of the play: Em Stott, Jessica Clark, Natalie Simpson and Jenny Rainsford.

To the glorious collaborators who have helped bring this play to life: TD, Jules, Naomi, Nao, Katie, Beth, and Delphine, thank you for your ideas, questions, and incredible imaginations. Thank you to the backstage teams and to Joni for keeping us going.

To Rebekah, Tanya and Letty, you have overwhelmed me every day with your generosity, patience, talent and hard work. Thank you.

Thank you Mum and Dad, for your support from afar.

Thank you to my friends. In particular to Sarah, Letty, Theo, Ragevan, Ollie, Francie, Steph, Sam, Marietta, Bertie, and Marek, for keeping me upright.

Thank you to Tash, for being by my side for this past decade. I thank my lucky stars that I found you. And to Vanessa, for building me. You have no idea how much your friendship has grown me up, opened me out and helped me find some kind of happiness. I love you.

And my final thank you goes to possibly the greatest person ever invented/a side of the sun, Lucy Morrison. This play exists because of you. My gratitude for what you have done for me knows no bounds. Thank you most of all for being my friend.

Characters

.

Louise 'Lou' Hough
twenty-four

Isobel 'Tosh' Mackintosh
twenty-four

Fran 'Fran' Kennedy
twenty-four

A Boy

SCENES WITH GIRLS

'Poor girls. The world fattens them on the promise
of love. How badly they need it, and how little most of
them will ever get.'

Emma Cline, *The Girls*

'The precedents for the government of England
during the king's absence are not clearly known.'

B. Wilkinson,
Constitutional History of Medieval England

'Men are surprisingly essential,
you'll realise when you get one.'

Your mum

Notes

All scenes take place in the lounge which leads out to an adjoining bathroom.

Lights between scenes fall and rise quickly, breaking directly in to and out of conversations.

Generally, punctuation indicates speech pattern.

/ indicates overlapping dialogue.

Words in [brackets] are unsaid, or surmised non-verbally.

Ha ha is 'Ha ha'. Laughter is laughter.

This play is full of moments of strange and deliberate gesture. Some of these are precisely described. But there is also space in the play for more to be found by the actors.

There are several 'Hooptedoodles' in this play. These are moments that exist outside of the narrative, designed to provide additional life in the world of the characters, additional space for the characters to breathe. These can be moved as desired or omitted entirely.

SCENE ONE

Two young women. Sitting.

*The lounge of the flat they share. Fairly ordinary. Some
effort. Some items of beauty and pride. Items with
meaning attached. Items left by dissenters. A muddle of
the stuff of people living separate together lives. Home.*

*Right next to the lounge is a small bathroom, which
can be accessed through a door to the landing.
Conversations can be had seamlessly between the lounge
and bathroom with just a slight raising of the voice. The
bathroom is fine, a bit scummy.*

*Both women are often on their laptops or phones.
Whether beside them or in their laps. Scrolling, clicking,
working, half-reading.*

*Lou is very animated as she talks. A louder voice than
anyone in the room. A sense she is always about to get up
and do something other than just sit and talk to you. Tosh
is a little odder, more awry, less comfortable in her body.
Possibly magical? Possibly a monster from the deep. She
follows Lou intently, offering anything she can to support,
encourage. They communicate very, very, very quickly.
They are completely in sync. Their conversation dances.
Time together is like a collective reverie.*

And –

Tosh that's quite strong

Lou I mean I must've been fairly keen because we don't
even leave we just hunker down and doink in some kid's
room

Tosh shwing shwing

Lou Like I get a Polly Pocket or some shit embedded in my thigh

Tosh laughs briefly.

And he is a big lad by the way –
    I mean *I* look like a Polly Pocket in comparison to his Heft

Tosh what number are we on now?

Lou Twenty-Three, Twenty-Four if you count Twenty-One-Point-Five which I don't cos that was largely / oral

Tosh largely oral, yeah

Lou Anyway anyway –

Tosh can I just get some water

Lou You would've HATED everyone at this thing, Tosh
    It was human tapioca

Tosh laughs.

A vortex of shit chat and bodycon

Tosh lets out a bigger squeal of a laugh.
    Lou comes onto her knees, performs for her. Tosh mirrors.

Flapjacks of make-up
    Scents Of Sandalwood
    Fucking Gender Everywhere

Tosh laughs, sucks in Lou's description like delicious foodstuffs off her fingers.

The *lack of imagination* was oppressive – Like everyone was just desperate to remind each other of their *diametric* genital qualities

Tosh oof – (*Through hand trumpet.*) TRIPLE WORD SCORE

They high five, Tosh retains their hands in the air.

Lou I mean it's all very fucking ordinary but all the tit tape is staring at me like I've just – taken a dump on the floor I'm that objectionable

Tosh and how long untillll

Lou's phone buzzes.

Lou I'm a touch Marissa by this point but still predominantly vertical

Tosh season two or three

Lou Dead in three, hun

Tosh oh yeah sad times

Lou I'm not dead yet I'm like one-bottle drunk. Once I'd decided I needed to fucking rouse myself

Tosh So you decided.

The briefest of beats.

Lou Yeah?

Tosh Great

Lou's phone buzzes twice. She checks it seamlessly throughout the next.

Lou I mean I keep having the same fucking, conversational equivalent of a – nosebleed in a swimming pool and I think I think I need to fuck all the WORD out of me

Tosh Okay, and is he

Lou I mean I've been bleeding so much lately it's strange to get my head round to the idea of myself as available for entry but I try my best

She winks.

Tosh Oop!

Phone down.

Lou And maybe I was,
   Emboldened by the challenge?

Tosh that's hilarious

Lou To find potential in this sea of – assembled curd

Tosh That is a hilarious thing you just said, I find that hilarious

Lou So when this boy pops up

Tosh who, Munch Bunch

Lou (*immediately points and clicks at Tosh*) Fun.

Tosh (*immediately reciprocating the gesture*) FUN.

Lou (*immediately back in –*) so when this boy pops up and basically estimates that I'm the most promising prospect there –

Tosh does a little dance on –

Tosh Understandably

Lou I figure –

Tosh You are *very promising*

Tosh is still dancing.

Lou thank you – I figure I might as well go with him, right,

Tosh right

Lou for the / Story

Tosh The Story, right

Lou So I don't actually judge myself, y'know?
   I don't actually have any post-partum guilt that I chose this human bagel of a boy to bang

Tosh A bagel? Oh he was round sorry / sorry

Lou No it was like, the quality of his skin, the texture of / it

Tosh Riiight right right right / riiiight

Lou He was a hunk in every possible sense of the word except for the word 'Hunk'

Tosh Totally get you.

Lou suddenly stands. She is a little tentative, modest.

Lou And go with me on this

Tosh I'm going

Lou Cos I don't mean to sound like up my own arse
But he was like *a little bit thrilled* to be getting with me?

A very, very brief pause.

Tosh Well duh

Tosh rubs her nose aggressively.

Lou Was that a bit [immodest]?

Tosh You're only the greatest person ever invented and he's some boy who's probably never had a conversation with a side of the sun before –

Lou to be fair

Tosh – but like *Let's Be Modest About It*

Lou To be fair he had A Nice Way.

Tosh looks at Lou. A pause.

No. No, he was just a potato cut-out, obviously, Sorry

Tosh You're welcome
I mean –
You're forgiven.

A brief pause.

Lou It was weird.

A pause.

Lou's phone buzzes. She just holds it.

like when he finished, I got that thing

Tosh What thing

Lou That thing y'know when you wake up in the morning and you've got a dead / arm?

Tosh A dead arm, oh I hate that

Lou Well I had that, but everywhere

Tosh thinks.

Tosh A Dead Everywhere.

Lou Yes.

Lou's phone buzzes. She checks it.
A pause as she does this. Tosh waits. She flips her phone over and back over face down again.

Tosh Right –

Phone away –

Lou And you know I know 'mindfulness' is like next-level middleagedlady bullshittery

Tosh Total gunt chat, yes

Lou points at Tosh.

Lou But I think I might've like. Got it?

Tosh What?

Lou thinks.

Lou I mean. I could barely feel him go in.

Tosh that sounds . . .

Lou I mean it was extraordinary.
I mean it was – *troubling* –

A pause.
Tosh nodding a bit.

But in a way that was – extraordinary.

A pause.

Tosh right

Lights fall.

SCENE TWO

Lights up immediately. Tosh and Lou are in exactly the same position as before.
Tosh is animated. Immediately –

Tosh so he's pounding away

Lou rum puppa pum pum

Tosh And at the moment of impact

Lou yeah

Tosh he explodes

Lou yeah

Tosh into a shower of confetti, pink and white confetti, that covers me, head to toe
And I lie there for a moment in it

Lou okay

Tosh And then I suck it all up, into my mouth like a hoover
And I chew it up and spit it out and mould the goop into little statues of Russian dictators.

A slight pause. Lou looks at Tosh's 'creations'.

Lou Ooh a little spitty Putin

Tosh A little spitty Stalin
A little –

. . .

Actually I can't think of any others but just imagine them all lined up and they look Russian.

They look at the statues.

SEX.

Tosh does a little flourish.
She then decapitates them all. Lou laughs.

So that was, Thursday

Lights fall.

SCENE THREE

Lou is animated, hovering about on foot.
Tosh is sitting.

Lou 'Whose pussy is this? Whose pussy is this?' he kept asking over and over

Tosh Classic

Lou I mean

Tosh that's Classic

Lou And I think he just wanted 'Yours, yours, yours' but I got a bit lost in the uh uh uh Philosophy of it

Tosh okay

Lou Like I wondered in that moment if it *was* mine, or if it was his, or no one's, *it was The Sex's.*

Tosh The what?

Lou The Sex's.

Tosh The Sex's

Lou Anyway I'm too preoccupied with that bombshell to even think about pretending to come

Tosh It was *The Sex's*?

Lou So I just lay there limp like a like a
/ Thumb?

Tosh Piece of bread?

Lou Bread I-FUCKING-love-you Bread –

    Tosh grins.

I'm a piece of bread And I look down at him,
    hard at work
    and looking so *meaningful* about it
    Not looking me in the eye *once*
    Just consistent fucking commitment to the goods
entrance

Tosh right also / lol

Lou and I think I should be thinking, Look at me. Look At Me,

Tosh (*repeating*) Look at me

Lou Cos I normally need the boy to look me in the eye, cos it reminds me they're all fucking . . .

    She searches for the right word.

Tosh / Fallible?

Lou Human.
    What?

Tosh Fallible.

    Beat.

Lou Oh yes no I like your word better. It reminds me they're all – fallible.

Tosh (*bit concerned about this*) Is fallible the right word actually?

She googles it.

Lou (*huge*) But this time I *didn't* need it. I had this Thought.

Tosh (*reading off the screen*) 'capable of making mistakes or being wrong'
Well duh-doi. I hate it when the definitions go (*Gestures inwards.*) that way instead of (*Gestures outwards.*) that way

Lou is waiting.

Sorry.

Lou I had this Thought.

Tosh (*shoulders up*) I love it when you Think

Lou (*shoulders up*) Big Thought

Tosh Was it about Sex?

Lou looks at Tosh. Drops her shoulders.

Lou Well, yeah.

Tosh No, I know I [was just being facetious lol sorry]

Lou puts aside her laptop and comes and sits right next to Tosh. She really wants to communicate this.

Lou I thought. What if I don't even want eye contact.
Like what if, this whole time. I've just been, what's the like Word word you're always like – 'conditioned'

Tosh (*nodding*) 'Conditioned'

Lou I've been 'conditioned', right, as a woman, to think that it's important, for me to have eye contact. Affection. To feel, to feel,

Tosh Connected

Lou *Right*, and I've never actually considered whether or not I want to be *not*

Tosh Connected

Lou Yeah, not in the room, like, *not in the room*

Tosh not in the room

Lou No, I mean, not, so, present

Tosh Wait, what do you mean

Lou What?

Tosh What do you mean, *exactly*, by that
     'Not in the room' 'Not Present'

Lou Like. Not. Present. *Not.*

Tosh No sorry I'm just trying to interrogate what you're saying as we go instead of just 'uh yeah' 'ah yeah' and not ingesting any of it

Lou Ah, lol I'm with you Thank you

Tosh Ah no probs probs

  Lou is momentarily distracted by her phone.

Lou What's the name of that thing that like shoots tennis balls out of itself?

Tosh I dunno. Why?

  Lou looks back at her phone.

Lou Cos I'm trying to make a joke.

  She thinks for a moment.

Fuck it – I've been too funny anyway –
   I'll just –
   (*Barely audible, while typing.*) 'hahahaha good wkend?'

23

She throws her phone across the room suddenly.

I fucking need the toilet AGAIN WHY

She goes to get her phone.

fuck I'm lonely

A brief pause.

Tosh hi

Lou puts her phone down.

Lou Sorry sorry thank the good hot lord for you

Tosh does a little spin, perhaps a 'yeee' –

So yes I've been investigating

Tosh Whah?

Lou The not-feeling feeling

Tosh Oh right yeah

Lou and there are people who
Like they're aware it's their body but they're not really
in it – Have you read about this?

Tosh No?

Lou It was on that group I'm in
The one where everyone posts pictures of their tits

Lou's phone buzzes.

Tosh Oh right yeah

Lou Aren't you on that one?

Tosh No I'm not no My groups are all verbal

Lou Well suddenly this thread popped up –

Lou's phone buzzes twice. She looks at it.

Tosh Is it just tits or the whole fucking gym display?

Lou is typing. Tosh waits.

Lou It's not pornographic. It's in the pinned post.

Tosh 'K

Lou So there's this whole thing about it, anyway, This whole like 'Movement.'

Tosh Oh right

Lou To Reduce Emotional Intimacy By Reducing Reliance On

Tosh Tits

Lou Are you even listening to me?

Tosh Yes. I'm just. Lost.

Tosh puts her laptop to one side.

Lou The idea is that you could be anywhere, and they could be anyone, and it doesn't matter at all because you're not present

Tosh But you are. You are actually / present

Lou is frowning.

Lou It's not important

Tosh But it is possibly relevant.

A brief pause.

Lou You're not judging me are you?

The briefest of pauses.

Tosh Literally no not never.

Lights fall immediately.

HOOPTEDOODLE ONE

Lou typing on her phone. Content silence.
    Tosh flips her phone over and over again several times.
    Tosh drags the screen down, as though to engender contact.
    After a moment she looks up at Lou as she does it, absently.
    Lights fall.

SCENE FOUR

Lights up almost immediately.
    Tosh and Lou are doing hip raises. Tosh is shit at it. She's mostly horizontal with the occasional brief erratic explosion of hip activity.

Tosh I'm playing that spool over and over in my head
    Will you be upset if I leave
    Will you. Be upset. If *I* leave
    Y'know trying it out in different, different

Lou Intonations

Tosh Yeah –

Lou The presumption of it is so annoying
    (*Voice.*) Like we actually want them there clamming up the bed

Tosh Yeah right so I get the head between my thighs
    And I start to crush right?
    And he's sort of Henry by this point

Lou What?

Tosh The Eighth

Lou Oh right yes
    And are you –

Tosh Anne Boleyn, yeah,
    I mean I know it's a bit of an obvious choice

Lou Right

Tosh I know we know this but sometimes I have to
repeat it to myself that this is the uh legacy of like all the
li'l boys sitting on bean bags playing Mario Kart

Lou I'm thinking we're getting off-topic

Tosh Sorry I didn't mean to bring All Of That in

Lou makes a gesture: 'No worries.' Tosh sits up.

So I just

*She touches Lou's hips gently, to stop her moving.
Reverence, please.*

I say her last words in praise of the king
    And I take his head clean off his shoulders.

A brief pause.

Lou And did that make you feel better.

Tosh Well, this is the thing, after all the gunk and
expected stuff came out there was this bunch of flowers,
    Sprouting right out of his spinal cord.
    And.
    And they were so beautiful

She is taken, briefly, then –

They smelled like citrus like Holiday
    So I put them in a mug by my bedside table
    Isn't that amazing? I mean can you believe that?

*A brief pause.
    Tosh is shining.*

Lou Yep yes

Tosh I can't believe they came out of him so beautiful
I was so sad when I woke up and they weren't there

A brief pause.

Lou Yeah. Wow.

A pause.
Lou carries on her hip raises.

You're so creative, Tosh. And you've got such a nice face.
I think it sometimes. I look at you and I think I have to
remember to tell you that.

Tosh is briefly overcome.

Tosh Oh that's nice. That's nice thank you.
PS I love you

Lou grins brightly at Tosh as she says –

the book and not the major motion picture

*Lou claps index fingers together in a mini round of
applause.*
Tosh waits.

Lou Oh god, ditto yes. Goes without.

Tosh nods. Lou carries on raising her hips.

Tosh But do though.

Lou (*hips erect*) Of all the gin joints in all the world you
had to fart into mine

Tosh laughs. They point at each other.

Tosh / YOU

Lou YOU

Tosh laughs, clambers onto Lou.
Flops about a bit.
Lies flat across her, suddenly somewhat despondent.

Tosh Do you think she went to heaven? Anne?

Lou What? Oh, er, no I don't believe in / the afterlife

Tosh I think I entirely crack open my belief system for the chance for Anne Boleyn to freely pass through to the other side
My li'l frightened, barren thing
I feel pointlessly connected to her –

Lou My fave's Jane Seymour

Tosh – I want a T-shirt with her face on it
Can you get those?

Tosh reaches for her laptop, it's too far. Gives up. Lies flat.

Lou Twenty-Three was called Henry.

Tosh doesn't say anything.
    Lou laughs a little.

He was pretty disollusioned about his monastery.

Lou laughs a lot.
    Tosh is quiet, smiles.
    Lou stops laughing into the quiet.

Come on that was excellent.

Lou is smiling. Tosh looks at her.
    Lights fall.

HOOPTEDOODLE TWO

Tosh and Lou are laughing in the bathroom.
Perhaps brushing their teeth.
Really laughing at something.
Then –

29

Tosh YOU'RE BEAUTIFUL

Lights fall.

HOOPTEDOODLE THREE

Lou falls, buckling into Tosh's arms. Kind of properly scary and awful. Total pain, a rare sight. Angry crying, hacking coughs. Her articulateness ebbs and flows with force. Tosh rubs her back, offering supportive 'mm' noises. This is a painful sight for her.

Lou 'ooh you're not like other girls',

Tosh mm, / cos you're not

Lou then they just go right on their merry way back to their other girls their (and you know I'm like opposed to this term) but their Basic girls
their *boring* fucking *boring as fuck* basic Lacoste Touch of Pink girls

A laugh accidentally escapes Tosh. Then she continues the appropriate 'mm's.

'You're so clever – the way you talk – you challenge me'
they want me to challenge them and I don't exist to challenge them

Tosh (*a hurt sound*) ow

Lou I mean I don't even *want* monogamy I'm not even *doing* monogamy

She hacky coughs –

Like maybe there's a little Lou inside who just wants to be held and fucking have a a a fucking cheese sandwich on the sofa with someone who's all, y'know, all in and shit but right now, right at this moment I'm just like I'm just like – no no no no – no, boy – no, boy – No.

30

Tosh is nodding ferociously.
   Lou suddenly sits up.
   Tosh is a bit disappointed.

Maybe I should just date girls but I already feel such a fucking responsibility to my gender the idea of dating one of my own I mean I'd just forgive them for everything.

A pause.

'You've been through a lot, babe'.

A brief pause.
   Tosh doesn't 'mm'.
   Lights fall.

SCENE FIVE

Lou is upright, bright, engaging. Tosh is waning.

Lou I mean I don't intend to be a fleshlight
   A Doll
   A fucking
   Wipe-Clean Person but
   I'm just really into this idea –
   The idea of not being completely in your own body
during

Tosh Absolutely

Lou is very momentarily distracted by her phone. And then –

Lou Like so it's

Tosh suddenly gets up and walks out of the room to the toilet. This doesn't alarm Lou. They continue the conversation without break, with just a slight raising of the voice.

so it's about not being completely, being completely not in *your* own body

Tosh Not being *completely*, or being *completely* Not

A pause.
Lou looks at her laptop. She types something. Tosh waits.

/ Not being –

Lou I think it's the first one!

Tosh Not Being Completely?

Lou clicks. Yes.

Lou Yes!

Tosh Right!

Lou's phone buzzes.

Lou Yes. Yes I think that's what I'm saying. Cos for the second one you would be like

Tosh You'd be like / Dead

Lou Dead.

They both laugh, alone, together.

Tosh Right. Got it. Deffo.

A brief pause.

Lou / WILLEM DAFOE

Tosh WILLEM DAFOE

They laugh again.
Tosh flushes the toilet. She turns the tap on and off. She stands, absently.
A pause.
Tosh looks at herself in the mirror, hard. Points an angry little finger.

(*Quietly loudly.*) NO.

She turns around from her reflection.
Lou suddenly laughs.

Lou (*raised voice*) I don't want to be a bitch but (*Salute.*) Number-One Girlfriend needs to stop posting pictures of pasta

Tosh rolls some toilet paper round her hand.

Tosh (*unheard?*) I thought she didn't exist any more

Lou (*raised voice*) It's just a constant stream of lactose-free-lasagne and wraparound sunglasses

Tosh Since she went to the dark side with Boyfriend, I thought she didn't / [exist]

Lou (*raised voice*) Why do they wear those wraparound sunglasses?

Tosh (*raised voice*) They must be streamlined-at-all-times!

Lou laughs, unheard.

(*Louder, again.*) They must be streamlined-at-all-times!

Lou (*louder*) Ha-HA!

A brief pause.
Lou's phone buzzes.
Tosh re-enters, yawning, holding her toilet paper.
Lou looks up at her.

I love her, but –

Tosh I thought she didn't exist any more.

Her mouth remains open, beast-like, tongue out for a moment.
She snaps it shut.

Since she entered the era post-boy

Lou frowns, still looking at the screen.

Lou Well, no she's not Post-Boy, she's very much, *in the midst of boy*, if you will, *we're* Post-/Boy

Tosh No I didn't mean like 'Post-Boy' I meant like post-boy, like since she's had, boy in

Lou doesn't make any attempt to understand.

Lou What was I talking about?

Tosh wanders out again.

Tosh You were talking about Sex!

Lou (*raised voice*) Right. Not being completely in your own body.

Tosh rolls her forehead across the door a few times.

(*Raised voice.*) Cos like I love sex but like I don't even need to be particularly present in the act?

Tosh / You don't?

Lou (*raised voice*) Cos therefore I am not done to therefore *he* is not doing to

Tosh / You don't.

Lou (*raised voice*) cos you like can't empower or disempower if there is there is no Subject d'you know what I mean?

Tosh flushes the toilet. She flips the tap on and off a few times.
A pause.

(*Raised voice.*) Do you know what I mean, Tosh?

Tosh comes back into the room. Lou looks up at Tosh.

Tosh That was like squeezing out a Fruit Shoot.

Lou (*accusing*) Do you know what I mean?

A brief pause.

34

Tosh Yes.

Lou I'm just doing so much other stuff at the moment that's new, that's unusual for me, and it's going so well, that maybe I only do things that feel unusual now

Tosh Yeah, I get that

Lou Because otherwise it's it's it's just like I'm just not really doing anything at all, I'm just being fucked.

A pause.

Being fucked shouldn't just be usual.

Tosh shifts into the room a bit.

Anyway / it's all –

Tosh So you've / forgiven them then

Lou Oh sorry

Tosh Sorry you go

Lou Oh –

Tosh So you've –
No, you go

Lou I was just gonna say it's all interesting. It's *all* learning.

A pause. Nodding.
Tosh goes to speak. Fails.
Lou taps away on her laptop.
Some moments.

So. How are you?

Tosh looks at Lou. A moment.

Tosh I'm fine. I mean. I'm not dehydrated.

A normal pause.
Lights fall.

35

SCENE SIX

Exactly the same position.

Lou He tasted like omelette.

A void.

It was so funny, I couldn't work out what it was and then we went for breakfast and I was like / – oHHH

Tosh (*almost involuntarily*) Sorry sorry can we stop talking about cock for a second?

Lou What?

A pause.
  Tosh covers her mouth, a little alarmed at what came out. She then uncovers it.

Tosh Sorry I just feel like my head's full of willy?
  Everything that's going in and out is willy?
  I haven't even seen one in two-and-a-half years and I still feel like I'm *choking* on –
  Sorry.
  Sorry?

A brief pause.

Lou No that's fine.

Tosh Sorry.

Lou No that's fine.

Tosh Sorry.

A pause.

Lou What should we talk about?

Tosh Politics.

Lights fall.

SCENE SEVEN

Lou and Tosh are standing. Game faces. Bit panicked.
Lou is holding her phone, waiting for messages.

Lou Literally no idea, my mind's like made up about five possibilities and they're all fucking nuts

Tosh I thought she didn't exist any more

Lou Why does she do this?

Tosh Since she left us for Thingy, I thought she didn't –

Lou Why does she suddenly pop up saying she 'has to talk to me'?
　You know how stressed I get when people say they need to talk to me

Tosh I know

Lou They should just fucking talk / to me

Tosh Talk to you, I know

Lou yells at her phone.

Lou STOP SENDING ME TONGUE EMOJIS AND GIVE ME A HINT, FRAN

Tosh stares at Lou's agitating.

Tosh I don't think I want her in our home actually.

Lou is messaging on her phone throughout the next.

Lou Used to be her home

Tosh No. She barely unpacked.

Lou smirks.

This was just a – holding area for her pants during her forcible, love-falling

Lou (*on phone*) That's quite a good sentence did you think that up in advance?

Tosh Umm

Lou suddenly looks up from her phone.

Lou Maybe she wants to have a faith chat again

Tosh When have we ever facilitated a successful faith chat

Lou We had that dinner?

Tosh Yeah / but

Lou We had that dinner where we said we'd make a / Concerted Effort

Tosh Concerted Effort, yeah, and then you said that Little Mix concert was like a Messianic experience and she cried? Do you remember that bit?

Lou makes a noise and then –

Lou Maybe they're breaking up

Tosh Maybe he died

Lou gasps.

Lou He choked on his lasagne

Tosh On all his Language

Lou laughs.

Harry Potter and the Chamber of fucking Language

Lou laughs harder.

I bet he's just asked to incorporate some light ass-play into proceedings and she wants us to do our feminist jiggery-pokery on it to make it acceptable

Lou lol at the words 'light ass-play'

Tosh she shouldn't be allowed though.

Lou (*ignoring her*) Oh my god if she's asking me to be a, bridesmaid or something I'm going to throw up a fucking kidney

Tosh D'you reckon?

Lou (*to herself, hard*) No, he wouldn't marry her

A bit of a pause.
  Tosh looks at Lou, who is a bit lost in this last point.
  Suddenly scared.

Tosh Let's cancel, actually. Blame me. Say I've got rickets. I never eat your fucking satsumas.

Lou Nah we can't do that she's like our best friend.

Tosh No, actually.
  (*Harder.*) She shouldn't be allowed.

Lou looks at Tosh, cheeks inflated.

I know she wants to prove how rad she is now
  But I don't think you should be allowed to reject our world to find our world despicable and then be like welcomed back with open arms every time you get bored of talking to your boyfriend
  I mean.
  Don't you have to earn. This?

Lou isn't really listening. She is reading back over messages.

Lou What does that mean Earn what

Tosh gets a bit stampy.

Tosh This?
  To be part of the Circle don't you have to
  Be part of the Circle?

Lou thinks.

39

Lou Circle sounds a bit oppressive

Tosh Fuck off you know what I mean Sorry I said fuck off

Lou It's okay.
   Are you okay?

Tosh I just –

   Tosh makes an aggravated noise.
      Lou waits, conscious of messages piling into her phone.

When has she ever engaged with our actual lives?

Lou I know

Tosh Since Boy when has she ever affirmed or supported our – fucking – ass-play?

Lou I know, I'm – agreeing with you

Tosh We're not just sediment we do exist beyond our affirmative language

Lou To be fair she asks you about your thesis. She's definitely tried to engage with your thesis, she printed out all that Rupi Kaur,

   Lou going to the door.
      Tosh thinks very hard, fists claw-like.
      She produces her lump of coal –

Tosh What about Four. Tearing at my tits outside Sainsbury's?

   A judder to a halt.

Lou (*unconvinced*) Did he?

Tosh He was on a mission for breasts that night I don't think my face even factored into it I think he actually covered my face with his hand

Lou Oh yeah, that's

Tosh Exactly, and I've never even talked about that.

Lou Yeah, that's.
That's.

A pause.
Lou is a bit unsure.

Did you want to – talk about that now?

A brief pause.

Tosh No I just.

A brief pause.

(*Quietly.*) I have stuff too.

Lou looks at Tosh.

Lou I know.

Lou's phone buzzes. She turns the buzzer off
immediately.

Tosh I just think we need to get some shit sorted before
we cancel all our plans to sit here and listen to her talk
about her fucking nothing.

A brief pause. Tosh faintly breathless.

Sorry.

Lou It's okay.

Tosh I do quite love her

Lou I know

Tosh I might just have to button it cos otherwise I'm
going to bitch out

Lou Okay. Okay well maybe you do that.

Tosh Yeah.

Lou We'll just get her in, get her out, shake shit all about.

Tosh Yeah.

Lou I love you

Tosh Yeah

Lou We'll debrief later.

Lights fall.

SCENE EIGHT

Fran and Tosh and Lou. Tea. Fran has an uncomplicated brightness to her that shines out. She wants to have a nice time, quite a lot of the time. A sense she is in a slightly different conversation to the one that is being had in this room –

Lou Yeah I mean I got like a *Polly Pocket* or some shit embedded into my thigh

Fran laughs.

And he was such a big lad I mean *I* looked like a Polly Pocket in comparison to him

Fran laughs, more, genuine.

Fran Oh my god, that's so funny!

Lou I mean like, this man / got Heft

Tosh Got Heft

Fran laughs.

Fran Youjustsaidthatatthesametime/that'sfunny

Lou So I lay there totally limp, like a piece of bread
I mean

Fran Ha-ha! Bread!

She laughs.

Lou I mean he left *impressions* in me

Fran explodes –

Fran Oh my god! That's such a weird image?

Lou But I got that thing
You know that thing like when you wake up and you
feel like dead everywhere?

Fran's laughter wanes, still smiling.

Fran What?

Tosh Like a Dead Arm

Lou Right right right but like everywhere

Fran (*smiling*) What? When do you feel like that sorry?

Lou is a little breathless.

Lou Like when you wake up in the morning and it's a
Dead Arm cos you've slept on it funny

Fran What?

Lou Like –

Fran It's dead?

Lou / Yes!

Tosh Yeah she had that right but like everywhere

Fran She's dead . . . everywhere

Lou claps and points at Fran.

Lou Yes!
Sort of!
Yes!

A pause. Fran waits for more.

43

It was like that, but everywhere, when he was fucking me.
Af-after he was, uh, fucking me. Dead Everywhere.
Because he was so fat!

Lou laughs. Tosh laughs, conspiratorial.
Fran smiles.

Fran Ohhh right! Oh yeah! I get it! Ha-HA! That's so –
So this was in the morning?

Lou No! Fucking –
No.
Never mind.
It was funny.

Fran Yeah.
It sounds. funny.

A pause.
Lou suddenly brightens.

Lou So how is it going then, Fran? With you and
Thingy?

Fran is visibly relieved.

Fran Yeah great thank you, we're like so happy and we
never argue.

Lights fall.

SCENE NINE

Lou is in the toilet. Fran and Tosh are sitting, politely,
silently.
A little phone alarm suddenly punctures the air.
Annoying. Fran suddenly springs into action, alert and
faffy, brings out her phone, turns the alarm off.
She brings up her bag, checks in the pockets, brings out
her Pill packet, a bottle of water. She checks the date of

44

her Pill methodically, unpackets it. Swallows it with water with some show.
    Tosh watches her with fascination.
    A pause. Fran swallows.
    She realises Tosh is just watching her, without shame.

Fran So, have you got any gossip?

Tosh does a 'That's absurd and hilarious' face. She then makes another face, as though trying to conceive of the absurdity.
    Fran just looks at her.
    This is the end of the conversation.

Sorry.

Lights fall.

Lou is back. She is sitting a little closer to Fran than before. Bright.

Lou You don't argue about anything?

Fran No. We like. We actually joke about what our first argument is going to be.
    Like if he's one day going to have an issue with my Japan thing, or.

Lou That's funny.

Fran He's so uncomplicated. Honestly. He's like a girl.

Lou Really?

Fran No I don't mean *like a girl* I mean like. In the way that he's kind and we share and he listens to me and we work through everything like logically like

Lou Laterally

Fran Right he's like laterally um so great and he loves me like a girl *and* a boy Like you guys, y'know?
The way you love each other
The full way

Lou The full way

Tosh Without the transaction

Lou What?

Tosh Sex

Lou Oh right yeah

Tosh Without the need for the transaction

Lou Oh wait do you guys not (*As if searching for a polite word.*) . . . bang

Fran No, no n-no he loves me like that too
So it's like your guys's love, it's like your love – Plus

A pause. Tosh and Lou exchange looks.

Gosh I'm making it sound really boring, aren't I?

Lou No, no

Fran The sex is still Amazing

Lou That's great

A pause. Nodding.

Fran Sometimes *we* have sex in the morning.
Sometimes we have it instead of breakfast.

Lou and Tosh look at her. Tiny smiles.

Lou Wow.

Tosh That's.

A brief pause.

Fran Yeah it's so

Fran tries for the word.

Hot

A wide-eyed pause.
   Fran is incredibly worried about what she just said.
   A few attempts to fill the pause.
   A longer pause.
   Tosh stands up, possibly aimlessly, possibly to go to
the toilet.

Are you seeing anyone?

Lou smiles. Tosh turns around on the spot, faces Lou.
She hides a smile. This is funny.

Lou Um

She shares a look with Tosh.

I mean, yeah, multiple

Tosh Well no

Lou looks at Tosh for a moment.

Lou Well yeah, no, I'm not like, 'seeing', I don't 'see'

A blank pause.

Tosh Yeah. We don't / see –

Tosh sits very close to Lou.

Lou I'm trying to like, uh de-uh-programme my, like,
y'know, away from the societal, y'know,
   (*To Tosh.*) babe can you, Blankety Blank my uh –

She leans on Tosh's shoulder, briefly tired.

Tosh We're trying to — deprogramme ourselves from the,
like, narrative that women have to – we've talked to you
about the Typical Narratives before, right?

Fran is briefly blank. Then –

Fran Yes.

Tosh So the narrative that women have to like devolve all their y'know –
   is 'devolve' the right word?

Lou Devolve?

Tosh Umm

   She googles it.

Lou devolve all my self-worth from

Tosh *our* / um

Lou right our interaction or non-interaction with –

   Tosh reads off her phone –

Tosh 'transfer or delegate (power) to a lower level'

Lou yeah of power to the boy as the sole uh, conduit of

Tosh *conduit*

   They both look at each other, do a hand-to-mouth pose.

/ Oop!

Lou Oop!

   They laugh a little, suddenly –

But yeah conduit of our self-worth.

   Tosh nods heavily.

Fran Oh, so you're both, doing that –

   Lou jumps forward a bit.

Lou Well, I'm being a bit more practical, Tosh is more in the – theoretical – that's right, right?

   Tosh is momentarily stunned. And then –

Tosh Uh. Yeah. Yeah.

A bit of a pause.
Tosh looks down at her wretched self.
Lou stands.

Lou Like I basically I basically want to deprogramme myself from the societal demand of male affection.

Like I want to deprogramme myself from the societal demand of wanting a cuddle.

Tosh looks up from her phone.
A brief pause.

Fran Wow. Well that's. Well that's amazing.

A pause.
Sipping.
Lou suddenly stands.

Lou I think the Pad Thais might be just about done.

Tosh Pad Thai Oh My

Lou sticks her tongue out at Tosh. Love.
Suddenly Fran explodes –

Fran We do sometimes argue.

Lou and Tosh look at her.

We do sometimes. Like there's a pushing, kind of thing

Lou Pushing?

Fran Non-physical obviously

Lou / Obviously, yeeshk

Tosh Obviously,

Fran Obviously

Lou (*to Tosh*) THIS IS / BRAND-NEW INFORMATION

Tosh BRAND-NEW INFORMATION

Fran smiles, unsure.

Lou Sorry, you argue

Fran I am sometimes a bit afraid that he's holding back on um. His true um.

Lou Yeah I was gonna ask, is there any holding back?

Tosh yeah

Fran Like he sometimes looks like he's going to um speak and then he sort of gathers me up in his arms and kisses my head and sort of unwraps and leaves me there.
    Does that sounds like a holding back to you?

A brief pause. Thinking.

Lou Maybe?

Tosh I mean it sounds / okay

Lou I think it depends on the moments immediately before and after where he's choosing not to speak
    Cos I assume he is choosing not to speak, right

Tosh Yes I mean based on what she's just told us, that's

Fran Well, yeah. No. I don't know –

Lou Look, he's a simple guy.

Fran He's not *that* simple, he's I mean he's a Physicist

Lou No but he's, he's

Tosh Uncomplex

Lou No he's uncomplicated

Fran Is there a difference?

Tosh No yeah there is actually, totally a difference, between uncomplicated and uncomplex

Fran And which one is good?

Lou It's not about good, hun

Fran Right but which one is, better?

Tosh / Uncomplex

Lou Uncomplicated

Fran Right.

A very brief pause.

Lou Look, he's a Textbook Nester.
Like he wants to make his / Nest

Tosh Nest, yeah

Lou And you don't need to worry. He's made his Nest.
And you're, like. In it.

A pause.

Fran Right.
Is that definitely enough for a person?

Tosh What?

Fran That?

Lou What?

Fran Me?

A pause.

Lou It's not just you. It's you and the whole surrounding
features of you. It's the fact that He Has You, *as well* as
the fact that he has you.

Fran What?

Tosh No I totally get that.

Lou and Tosh look at each other.

Fran I don't?

Lou A person to be with, to be a witness, to be a support

Tosh Proof

Lou Yeah. What?

Tosh Proof. That he's worth, like. Any time at all.

Lou Oh yeah. Oh *yeah*. Good one.

A pause.

Fran So the uh –

Lou You're fine, basically.

Tosh Yeah everything's fine. And you're loved.

Fran Oh, good. Good.
I feel better.
You girls are the best.

Lou Aw. Babe.

Fran I'm glad we had this chat.

A long pause. Sipping.
Then –

Oh my god I forgot! We're getting married! That's why I came round!

She laughs a bit.
Tosh and Lou sort of clap.

Lou Oh my god that's amazing!

Tosh Congratulations!

The noise dies down.
Fran is grinning, relieved.

Fran Ah I'm so – I'm so pleased you um –
I was sort of – nervous to tell you haha that's so weird!
Hahahah

Laughter dies down.
  Lots of nodding.

Tosh That's amazing. That's amazing though. / That's amazing though.

Lou That's amazing

Tosh That's amazing though

  Lights fall.

SCENE ELEVEN

Fran is gone. Tosh and Lou are standing. No laptops in sight. Gleeful, energetic, sweating. They are instinctively speaking covertly, slightly quieter than normal. Bitching voice, even though there is no one to overhear them.

Tosh That's all it is for her though

Lou Oh my god I'm so glad you said that I was starting to think it was just me!

Tosh Like I'm happy for her

Lou Oh my god absolutely
  So, like *so* –

Tosh *So*

Lou But I wouldn't choose that

Tosh Not for me thank yee

Lou Yeah

Tosh I mean, yeah

Lou I don't think I've ever met anyone so addicted to the Narrative

Tosh Oh my god she's High Fuckin' Sheriff of the Narrative

Lou Like I'm not completely sure if she has engaged with her imagination once.

Tosh I know

Lou I mean they don't *do* anything
They just sit around eating his lasagne

Tosh Eating all his Language

Lou laughs.

Lou She sort of *is* the human equivalent of a lasagne isn't she
A flappy, gutless

Tosh I mean they don't even *argue*

Lou Exactly exactly I mean you have to *do* something to each other. Otherwise it's just –

Tosh It's fucking nothing, it's just fucking and nothing

Lou She's too scared of him to argue.

Tosh She's too scared of *losing him* to argue

Lou I bet they don't even fuck, or well

Tosh (*unconvinced*) Yeah

Lou I bet he has to get written permission

Tosh Hah

Lou He is going to get bored of her.

Tosh frowns.

Tosh Well. Yeah, and he's –

Lou Like there's a point when you need more than a paper plate with a face drawn on it as your life partner

Tosh (*voice*) Yes And He's Also Quite Dull

Lou We're not biologically anatomically moulded for monogamy, you know

Tosh I know –

Lou I mean I didn't even read that on a group that was on Netflix
  This shit is mainstream now
  How dare she be so unintelligent about this?
  How DARE she be so – so UNINTERROGATIVE about this?

  Tosh is nodding, trying to keep up –

She's just choosing someone to watch her die now
  Instead of fully enacting the blind glorious thumping possibility of her biology
  She will never
  Ever
  Do anything of significance now.
  I want to yell it at her.
  I want to write on a cake in fucking fucking lactose

Tosh (*loudly, uncertainly*) Yeah no totally yeah

Lou She doesn't even dress well she doesn't even use conditioner she *puts her wet hair in a ponytail* and leaves the house and SHE'S THE ONE GETTING MARRIED I just I can't even –

  A brief pause.
    Lou takes a breath.

I could fuck him, right, full-bush crusty in some . . . roadside public toilet and it'd still be better than four hundred of the bone-dry bangs she gives him.

  A pause.
    Tosh frowns. She begins to cry, almost unnoticeably.
    Lou stares somewhere, hard.

No wait that's mean.

A pause.

I'm just really embarrassed for her.

Tosh stares at Lou. Lou crosses her face like a hard little shell.
   Lights fall.

HOOPTEDOODLE FOUR

Tosh and Lou are on their laptops.
   Tosh looks up at Lou. Lou looks at Tosh.
   Tosh sings.

Tosh EMOTIONAL MANIPULATION

They sing in odd harmony. Changing with every line, leading and following.

Tosh *and* **Lou** EMOTIONAL MANIPULATION
   EMOTIONAL MANIPULATION
   EMOTIONAL MANIPULATION
   EMOTIONAL MANIPULATION

Lou everything / hurts today

Tosh EMOTIONAL / MANIPULATION

Lou MANIPULATION

A pause.

Tosh *and* **Lou** EMOTIONAL MANIPULATION
   Lights fall.

Tosh and Lou are lying on the floor.
It is the middle of the night.
It is a sleepover.
Tosh is speaking freely.

Tosh and that that that that everything has been,
Made
like I sometimes will be there and suddenly, completely,
totally overwhelmed by like, the *toilet-roll dispenser*
beside me because that has been invented and brought
into the world because it has been *presumed to be*
necessary by someone somewhere and now it is part of
what it is to be human to use –
like a *bed* the idea of *bed* has been invented a bed has
been presumed to be necessary and now is.
And Money?
like, like, trams?
Straws?
chairs fucking CHAIRS?
socks?
marriage?
The Things??
christmas?
like someone's made *all of this up*
and it's become human
but what if what if none of it um.

Tosh picks a stray bit of fluff off Lou.
She thinks.

/ Has – to – be?

Lou But isn't it nice that don't you ever feel like it's all
sort of in around you and holding you and someone's
thought about all of it and it's all right.

Tosh [What?]

Lou Like it's all in around you and holding you. Like someone's thought all of this through for you.

Tosh doesn't say anything.

Like sometimes like even commerce isn't horrible because it just means everything's been catered to you. Like it loves you. That's really bad that I said that probably. But yeah.

A pause.
Lights fall.

SCENE TWELVE

Tosh is panicking in the bathroom, sat on the toilet lid.
Lou is on her laptop.
Tosh is surprised that Lou hasn't come to check on her.
After a moment she stands up and smacks the toilet lid down on the toilet seat with a thump.
Lou sits up. She picks herself up and goes to try the bathroom door, still holding her laptop. It opens a little and Tosh promptly pushes it shut.
Immediately –

Tosh I'm fine I'm fine I mean I'm doing a bit terribly but I'm fine.

Lou steps back from the door.

Lou Tell me what's happening, hun

Tosh sits on the toilet seat.

Tosh I'm totally fine just a boy fell into my head last night and knocked a few things over well it might've been it has a bow tie on that's boy innit I didn't catch the fucker –
But no sorry I'm fine
I think I'm just hungry

Lou That's okay, hun – do you want a snack?

58

Tosh Do you think I'm Mentally Ill?

Lou What?

A brief pause. Tosh waits.

Well possibly in a contemporary sense yes but not *actually* actually

Tosh There's only so many ways of saying it.
I lack, I lack, I lack.

Lou What?

Tosh I don't know.

Lou Okay.

A brief pause.

I can leave you?

Tosh (*quietly*) I'm not the Before, y'know

Lou What?

Lou goes closer to the door.

Tosh Before what's coming along. You're lucky I came along.

Lou What?

A pained pause.

Tosh Can you not hear me or do you not understand?

Lou I.
I can't hear you.

A pause.

What, Tosh?

A pause.
Tosh goes very close to the toilet door and leans her forehead against it. Lou listens from the other side.

Tosh I need the Proof, Lou.

Lou What's proof?

Tosh They're not *that* interesting you know
      They actually *do* smell and are worse
      Like there's a reason for those fuckingT-shirts

      Lou thinks.

Lou I'm sorry. Again. What?

Tosh Let's throw rocks at them!
      Let's
      Let's chloroform them tie them to a tree set fire to it!
      Yes, let's
      / Yes, let's
      Say it with me YES, LET'S

Lou Babe
      Babe
      Babe
      It's okay
      I know you feel weird about them

      Tosh jumps up and down –

Tosh THIS ISN'T ABOUT THEM

Lou Okay?

Tosh It's you!
      It's about you

Lou Okay –

Tosh Stop Being
      Casual

Lou I'm not

Tosh *Stop* looking over my shoulder

Lou I'm not!

Tosh opens the door to Lou. She looks at her, wearily,
but with love.

Tosh Can you just dig in, please?
Can you just hair up, pull on your joggers and dig
into us.

A pause.

Lou Okay.

Lights fall.

HOOPTEDOODLE SIX

Lou and Tosh are hugging each other.
Tosh is hugging very hard.
Several moments in silence.

Lou (*to indicate a need to move out of the hug*) Okay.

Lights fall.

SCENE THIRTEEN

Lou and Tosh and Fran.
Tosh is frowning, visibly retreated from the situation.
Fran is sitting, hands resting in her lap, pleasant, almost
formal.

Lou I've been looking into it and there's actually a place
in Brighton where they do a party every Thursday

A brief pause.
Fran doesn't quite know what to say.

Fran (*smiling*) That's an interesting choice of day.

Lou I know! I know. I think the point is that you don't
plan your whole weekend around it

Fran Mm

Lou Like so you can start to apply to it some normality

Fran Normality, yeah, that's

Tosh starts to eat at her hand.

Lou Like I think the idea is that everyone who goes to these things wants it to become a completely normalised part of their sexual routine

Tosh Holy fucking shit that's wild

A beat.

Fran Yeah that's so –

Lou Although to be honest I feel like it's getting a bit too normal
    Not *normal*, obv, I mean we're all fucking (*She gestures something abhorrent.*) but like, what's the word?

She looks at Tosh for support.

Tosh I don't know, at all

A brief, blank, blinking pause. Lou returns to the role of orator –

Lou Everyone's getting a bit *nice*, though
    There's so much *pleasantry* now
    It's really going downhill

Tosh When were you up – hill

Lou Like what is that about? Is this chronic need to piss all over each other some sort of patriarchal hangover?

Tosh starts slowly sinking into the couch.

Fran Hhha – that's so funny,

Lou It's all Bond Bond Bond
    Anti-Bond Anti-Bond *Bond*

Fran (*having fun*) Bond / bond bond bond

Lou Just generating parameters everywhere even in a parameter-free zone
    I just want to go to a grouping of people where everyone doesn't have to mean so fucking much to each other
    It's soooooooooooo lazy

Fran That's so funny

Lou Sorry can you stop saying That's so funny

A brief pause. Shock.

Fran I was just um active listening um showing I was listening

Lou Well could you do something else to show you're – ? Only it makes me think you're not really listening you're just saying That's so funny instead

Fran Okay, sorry

A brief puncture.

Lou What was I saying?

Fran You want a group where everyone doesn't rely on each other cos it's so lazy it's soooo lazy

Lou Oh right yeah

Fran (*quietly*) I was / listening

Lou Right, get this, there was some girl crying in the corner at the last night I went to because her non-exclusive cohabitation non-partner was Having A Non-Fucking fucking Verbal Conversation with someone else and that was Hers, apparently

Tosh rubs her nose ferociously.
    She starts crawling on the floor.

Everyone was like, patting her
   I honestly think people are like, trying to *date* in there
or something
   Like they go along trying to '*meet someone*'
   I'm so disappointed in all of them
   It's really going downhill, honestly

Fran is smiling, worried.

(*Laughing, not serious.*) Maybe I'm gonna have to start
dogging cos at least they wear masks

Tosh Oh my god
   OH MY GOD OH MY GOD

Everyone looks at Tosh.

Fran Are you okay, Tosh?

*Tosh pushes out her bottom lip for a moment: 'What to
do, what to do?'*
   Suddenly turns to Fran, hard.

Tosh Fran at school, were you one of the girls who talked
about snogging or about Assessment Objectives?

Lou Tosh

Fran Um. I – snogged.

Tosh smiles, nods.

Tosh And was this more interesting then?

Fran Um.

Tosh sniffs.
   *She suddenly gets up, walks out of the room,
slamming the door.*
   A hot pause.
   Incredibly still.

(*Mouthing.*) Is she all right?

Lou (*gesturing*) *She'll be fine*

Fran (*mouthing*) *Should we go after her?*

Lou (*mouthing*) *No, no just leave her, keep talking.*

Fran Um, so, um (*Mouthing.*) *Is she okay?*

Lou *Leave her, just keep talking*

Fran Um. At school we had a tally board in Nell Hobson's desk.

Lou Oh really? (*Mouthing.*) *What? keep going*

Fran Like a little Hangman sort of well Hangwoman sort of thing but where the boy had touched you – um. (*Mouthing.*) *Is it the wedding?*

Lou (*mouthing*) *NO, it's about me she's just sensitive about ME*

Fran (*mouthing*) *What?*

Lou (*mouthing*) *SENSITIVE just keep talking*

Fran Buuut but it got ruined cos girls used to make stuff up. Used to give themselves hickeys don't know how they did that.

Lou Top of a two-litre plastic bottle

Fran What?

Lou Coke or Highland Spring

Fran (*mouthing*) *Is it the virgin thing?*

Lou What?

Fran (*whispering*) *VIRGIN is it that?*

> *Tosh appears at the door suddenly, causing Fran and Lou to jump, and she says –*

Tosh At our school we used to sit on girls in the lower years, sit on them, hard, and make them describe a penis. Y'know the ones who swore they weren't fridges – and every time they got a bit anatomically wrong or whatever we'd smack them on the back of the neck with a Shatter-Resistant ruler. Did I ever tell you that?

Lou Yeah.

Tosh They nicked a Biology textbook out the science lab and would pass it round at break, revising, before we got to them. I still remember them all sweating.

A pause.

Fran That's so funny.
Sh[it].

She looks down, embarrassed.
    Lou's phone buzzes. She looks at it throughout the next.
    Tosh looks at Fran.

Tosh What happened to the first person who got hung please?

Fran What?

Tosh On Hangman.

Fran takes a moment to translate this.

Fran Well no one *actually* got –
    Actually this one girl said she got pregnant, but she was new, she came from quite a *normal* school so I think that one sort of backfired on her, actually.

Lou (*not looking up from her phone*) Lol.

Fran I remember her sitting in the corner at lunch just plating herself in the stomach.

Lou What?

Fran mimes ramming a plate into her stomach multiple times, laughs.

Oh right.

Fran Full view of the teachers. All turned out to be a lie in the end. I think she just wanted people to talk about her. She wasn't an interesting person.

A pause. Itchy.
Lou turns to Fran.

I remember when Sarah like got her on MSN and was like
R U A SLUT OR R U A LIAR
and she was just like –
Like –

A pause.
Fran does a :S face, with a sound.

Like the emoticon.

Fran laughs. Lou laughs.
A pause.

It was so funny. She like totally. Misunderstood. Like. How empowered we all were.

Tosh laughs at this.
Fran laughs too, unsure why.
Lou doesn't.
Fran stops laughing.
Tosh doesn't.
Lights fall.

SCENE FOURTEEN

Fran is gone. Lou is exercising. Little beats from her laptop. Tosh is standing, properly hard, full of internal pyrotechnics, outwardly still. Staring at Lou.

Lou is breathing quite heavily. Aware she is being watched.
Then –

Tosh What's that film?

A pause.
Lou turns her head to look at Tosh.

Lou Yeah gonna need a bit more than that.

A pause.

Tosh They fly.

A long pause. Lou is thinking, blankly.

Tosh Sunglasses

Lou Oh *The Matrix*.

Tosh Yep, right
It's like that.

A pause.

Lou What.
's 'like that'.

A brief pause. Tosh chooses her words.

What's wrong?

Tosh What?
Nothing's wrong. It's right
I mean I know Right doesn't exist any more but I think
I am, actually

Lou Okay

Tosh I've had a Thought.
Two Thoughts. Two Thoughts actually. Thoughts with
a capital Th.

Lou I love it when you Think

Tosh (*shut up*) AH – Number One.

She holds up one finger.

Sorry can you stop that FUCKING fucking thing sorry.

Lou slams her laptop shut and sits up. Tosh's finger is still aloft.

Number One.
Boys and girls are actually impossibly different things.

She pauses, for effect.

And I don't think we have the faculties to successfully align ourselves.

A pause.

Lou Do you want me to [respond]

Tosh No, just. That's Number One. Number –

Lou Just so you know, I don't understand, exactly, but

Tosh Two.

She holds up two fingers. A performance. A false start and then –

We have to stop. Like right now. Like right at this second.
And when I say we I mean you obv. I didn't want to be too aggressive and like, specific, I wanted to be gentle and, and general, but I mean *you*, actually, not generally, and very specifically, and not necessarily very gently.

Tosh holds her two fingers out for a little while, at Lou.

FUCKING. *STOP* IT.

The fingers hover, in mid-air, before –
Lights fall.

Lou and Fran are sitting.
    Tosh is lying horizontally back where she sits.
    A glass of water has been thrown over on the floor.
    An uncomfortable silence. A bomb has just gone off.

Fran Okay I'm gonna have a wee I think.

She gets up and goes to the bathroom.
    She goes on her phone on the toilet.
    Lou looks at Tosh for a long, still moment.

Lou That was quite strong. And quite loud. And quite unnecessary.

Tosh I want her to leave. And I want to talk to you.

Lou I don't think I want her to leave.

Tosh You can't keep inviting her round to provide a buffer she is not distracting enough

Lou I'm allowed to invite –

Tosh I've had this Thought

Lou No more Thoughts

Tosh Make her go. You hate her. Why do you always need a witness

Lou No I love her.

Fran flushes the toilet.

Tosh You cannot possibly love her. It is an impossible task. That is why. She is currently loved. By a fucking jar of pesto.

Lou involuntarily laughs. Stops herself.

Lou Shut the fuck up.

Tosh I'm convinced she must have drugged us for most of our voluntary friendship

Lou That's MEAN

Tosh YOU'RE MEAN WE'RE MEAN WE WENT TO GIRLS' SCHOOL IT'S IN OUR SKIN

Lou Oh my *god* Loud

Tosh (*mean*) Y'know I'm convinced she and him are just smooth down there, like Ken and Barbie, and they just frot their smooths together

Fran enters and comes to sit down.

until they are worn away. Like. Like.
(*To Fran.*) What's the opposive of concave?

Fran Um. Convex.

Tosh Right. Convex. To Concave.

Tosh does a little 'convex to concave' gesture with her hands. She does it again. She does it again.

Lou Stop it

Fran What are you doing?

Tosh Do it with me Fran. Do the thing.

Fran No?

Fran puts her hands up though.

Lou Stop it.

Tosh stops it.

Fran (*hands still in the air*) What's she talking about?

Tosh It's just a little stump now.

Fran What?

Tosh Whatever the stump equivalent of a fanny is.

Fran Oh, you're talking about sex.

Tosh Chup!

A brief pause.

Fran I'm going to have a [wee] –
Shit I just had one.

A brief pause.

Can I maybe go?

Lights change.
Fran collects her things and goes.
Tosh goes to the bathroom.
A door is slammed.
This can all still be happening as the next scene begins –

HOOPTEDOODLE SEVEN

Tosh bangs the toilet lid down once.
The sound pleases her.
She bangs it down thousands of times.
Lou panics.
Lights fall/change.

SCENE SIXTEEN

Tosh is in the bathroom. Lou is waiting outside the door.
Tosh knows she's there.
After a moment she opens the door.

Lou I think I need to say some shit to you.

Tosh pauses, blankly.

Tosh Why would you say that why wouldn't you just say your shit.

Lou A long time ago you told me to tell you if you started getting cunty.

Tosh thinks. She hoicks up her trousers.

Tosh No I'm almost definitely sure that wasn't me.

A pause.
Tosh walks past her into the living room, no intention behind the movement.

Lou You know I was reading it is possible to make yourself a kinder person. To make kindness your go-to.

Tosh If that was an attempt at subtlety. It wasn't really good enough.

Lou I need to say some shit to you.

Tosh Why would you say that why wouldn't you just say / your shit.

Lou Fine fucking. Here's the shit
I love you but

Tosh 'I love you but' is an unacceptable way to start delivering said shit

Lou You need to stop being so focused on me now.

Tosh thinks.

Tosh Nope.

Lou 'Nope' is an unacceptable way to receive my shit

Tosh All of this is for you
I've made myself normal about Them for you / do you even [know what that has taken]

Lou You're not normal

Tosh Fine fuck it what's normal in your –

Lou Like. *Being* normal. You don't react to or or say or do anything in a normal way

   Tosh opens her laptop.

Tosh I actually thought you didn't believe in normal sorry normative

Lou oh Fuck off

Tosh Everything is designed around facilitating your not version of normal sorry normative

Lou Okay okay on behalf of me, hiya, I relinquish you from the responsibility of facilitating / my

Tosh I forgive you, continually, every time we go round, in spite of / your reliance on

Lou Don't forgive me!

Tosh You need forgiveness you *need* to be / forgiven for

Lou No I don't!?!?!

Tosh You're not taking this *seriously enough*
   You're *not trying hard enough*

Lou Can I ask you something.

Tosh Why don't you just ask / it

Lou Can I ask you something.

Tosh Just fucking ask it don't

Lou Can I ask you something

Tosh Yes. Yes. Yes. What.

   Tosh closes her laptop and looks up at Lou, impatient.

Lou *Why* do you want me so much?

Tosh (*horror*) What?

74

Tosh almost malfunctions.

YOU'RE MY BEST FRIEND LOUISE YOU'RE MY /
PERSON

Lou You don't like anything that I say you are palpably
aggrieved by / everything I say

Tosh is glitching –

Tosh (*loud*) Why are you using the words / Palpably
Aggrieved

Lou You are Palpably Aggrieved by what I say you find
everything I care about trivial why are you so desperate to
keep me around

Tosh (*flippant*) I'm not! I'm fucking not!

Lou Y— you're not?

Tosh skitters, confused about what she's said too.

Tosh No! I mean –
Not like this!
There is a *better* version of this. I can see it.
I know you can't see it yet.
But I was thinking I could *coach* you

Lou just makes a sound.

To start to visualise a world without the boy in it
I think this is where it's all going anyway
I genuinely think in five to ten years we're going to
have several different possible 'happy's'

Lou What does that / even mean?

Tosh (*stressed*) Sorry, can you stop saying what?

Lou God I literally have got no idea what you're going to
say next. Like I need a What's amount of time to get to
grips with what you've just said before –

Tosh I don't think you used literally correctly

Lou Oh god Tosh can you not self-edit!

Tosh No I don't Like think I Like Can Like at Like All

Lou Oh suck my dick

Tosh No I will NOT suck your

Lou Oh MY GOD I WAS BEING FUCKING

Tosh You've become *so boring*

Lou stares at her.

Lou Don't say that to me.

Tosh You've become a parody. Hun. You're like the human equivalent of a Little Mix song.

Lou momentarily pauses.
    Tosh gets up, to go to the bathroom. To move, something.

Lou I *like* Little Mix!

Tosh is gesticulating wildly, offhand.

Tosh Me too! I love them! but there's a point when you have to realise you're just jumping up and down in a leotard yelling YOU MADE ME WHO I AM

Lou looks at Tosh.

Lou I need to say some shit to you.

Tosh suddenly turns and runs at Lou, who flinches and staggers back.
    Tosh stops dead in front of her.

Tosh Ugh I want to slap you but I'll do it wrong

Lou That's a wonderfully normal thing to say to a person

Tosh No you don't speak now.

She comes at Lou hard.

Whatever his love is, is crap.

It is worth crap.

I love you, and my love is worth much more. My love is solid fucking blood diamond compared to Twenty fuuuhcking whatever's fucking shit ass cruddy shitttttt shit SHIT love.

Lou goes quickly into the bathroom. Tosh pursues.

SHIT SHIT SHIT SHITTY LITTLE BOYS' LOVE HUN

Lou WHY do you even like me you don't even like who I am

She tries to slam the door but Tosh catches it.
Tosh joins her in there. She is suddenly calm.

(*Quiet?*) OH MY GOD YOU HAVE TO STOP

Tosh I have infinite value to you. I get barely anything out of this relationship, and he gets full access to your body and almost the entire contents of your head.

I don't even get a particularly large percentage of your concentration when I'm here.

Lou That's not true, you're eating my whole / life

Tosh I am sick of trying to persuade you that I'm worth as much energy as your boys. But I am. I am worth more because I receive less from you and yet I continue to contribute. I am keeping you alive. You need to keep me alive.

Lou doesn't say anything.

Aren't you bored? How haven't you got bored of it yet?

Lou (*quietly*) Just stop it a sec

Tosh Why isn't this (*Gestures.*) interesting enough for you?

77

Lou This is half of it, Tosh. I'm sorry.

  A brief pause.

Tosh No.

Lou This is literally like, half

Tosh (*suddenly enlivened*) Ooh *Do* you actually know what literally means?

Lou This is *literally half*

Tosh Half of what. What is the other LIT-ER-AL half.
  And don't say sex. If you say sex I swear to god I'll I'll
I'll I'll I'll fucking I'll

Lou What you'll what

Tosh Fucking THROW THINGS fucking THROW
THINGS. AT YOU fucking DIVORCE MY HEAD
FROM ITS BODY I'll just
  You can't
  (*Energetic, mental?*) *That* is not equally proportional
to, to *this*, *That* to *This*
  You can't say that
  IT MAKES ME WANT TO DIE WHEN YOU SAY
THAT

Lou Then Stop that Stop Wanting To Want That
  Cease / Cease Cease

Tosh YOU stop Wanting to Want, You need to stop
Wanting to Want

Lou Wait what?

Tosh The want the want
  Lou do you want or do you just want to be wanted

Lou I WANT TO BE WANTED
  I WANT TO BE WANTED
  FORGIVE ME YOU SPECIAL-NEEDS CHILD
  I WANT TO BE FUCKING WANTED

A brief pause.

Tosh Harsh.
Pretty harsh.
Actually.
Considering.
That.
I.
Basically raised you.

Lou Oh fuck off you didn't raise me

Tosh Built you. Built you, then.

Lou (*strong*) No.

Tosh When I met you you were shy. And pained. And full of spiders.
Then I. Just quietly, put myself next to you, and listened and accepted and promoted and fed and loved
and loved and loved and
Built a sparkling superhuman You.

A pause.
Lou's face flushes hot.
She shakes her head.
Tosh is light on her feet.

Lou You don't really have, like, Female Pain y'know.

Tosh turns back to her, interested.

Tosh I don't really have, like, Female / P—

Lou You haven't had enough interaction to have formed this much Pain.
You need to stop parading your Incel shit as wisdom you haven't even kissed someone sober.

Tosh I have so much wisdom it would make your blood fucking clot, hun

Lou Oh my GOD, Tosh

79

Tosh I am fucking. WISE

Lou No, no, you are frigid, that is what you are

A brief pause.
Tosh mock-gasps. Then –

Tosh Lol.

She smiles.

I'm not gonna call you one, you know.
    You want me to so badly but I won't do it.
    I know all you want in the world is to be a Whore but
you're so bad at it.

Lou *What?*

Tosh Sorry 'woman of ill repute'

Lou (*quietly*) What.

Tosh Sorry 'perpetually open garage'

Lou (*quietly*) Stop it

A brief pause.
Tosh reaches out an arm to Lou. Lou flinches a little,
but lets her.

Tosh You don't have to do it hun. You really don't have
to do it.
    I know you think it makes you interesting
    But it doesn't
    You are interesting *in spite of it*

Tosh brings Lou closer to her. Her speech is soft at first,
growing in triumph.
    Lou is spent.

I know you're collecting, you're still adding to your
Hangwoman – I know your number is your proudest
achievement you say it to yourself sometimes in the quiet
moments and feel as proud as when that girl asked

thirteen-year-old you if you were a fridge and you could
turn round and say
NO I am NOT I've had the middle and index fingers of
a BOY up me
I am NOT a fridge
I am NOT a fridge
I am TERRIBLY DESIRABLE

Lou Why are you being horrible to me?

Tosh I have never ever been horrible to you before and I
think that it's about time I was because it seems to be the
only kind of love slash attention you respond to.

A pause.

Lou That's –

Tosh looks down at Lou.

Tosh What happened in your early life that made you so
want the shitty version of love that they give you?

Lou That's horrible.

Tosh Yes. It is.

A substantial pause.
Tosh is really holding Lou upright now.
*Tosh suddenly drops her in the bathroom. Lou
stumbles a little, forward.*
Tosh sits down in the living room, opens her laptop.
Lou waits.
Lou goes into the living room and looks at Tosh.
Tosh doesn't look up.
*Lou goes and puts herself beside Tosh, a little
nervously.*
They stay like this for a moment.

Lou I hate boys.

A pause.

Tosh openly scoffs.

Tosh I hate girls.

They stay still for a moment.
Lights fall.

SCENE SEVENTEEN

Time has passed. Lou and Tosh are in precisely the same
position.
 Fran is there, sitting. Neither of them really look at her.
Tosh is still on her laptop. Bit bored.
 Lou is animated. Chatty, sort of happy.

Fran Well that's really modern.

Lou makes a happy sound.

Do you still get to. Um. [Have sex with boys]

Lou We're working out the parameters.

Tosh doesn't look up from her laptop. She occasionally
scratches the crap off her teeth.

We've got a list. On the fridge. So we can work it out,
make edits et cetera.

A brief pause.

We got one of those wipe-off whiteboard thingies.

Fran Oh. Smart.

A brief pause. Lou smiles up at Tosh.

Lou There's a point where you have to grow up and give
up the narrative. When it becomes unsustainable.

Tosh looks at Lou for a moment: 'What?' Lou notices.

Right?

A pause.
   Tosh is a bit tired. She considers her reply.
   She relents, smiles and nods, sympathetically(?).
   Goes back to her laptop.
   Lou hovers a little in space, waiting for greater
affirmation –

Fran It must feel really good to have, y'know. Worked all this out.

Lou laughs.

Lou Yeah. I feel like crazy good.

She breathes out, restored.
   A brief pause.
   Fran smiles.

Fran That's so funny. I mean Amazing. It's amazing.

A brief pause.

I mean I'm so happy for you.

A brief pause. Lou is looking at Tosh.

Lou Shall we get a Pad Thai when Fran's gone?

Tosh smiles a little. Lou waits.

Tosh (*half-arsed*) Pad Thai Oh My

Lou laughs, probably too much, probably a ha-ha.
   After she has finished the extent of her laughing,
Lou rolls her head to Fran.

Lou Sorry, Fran. We should probably, like, ask you a question.

Fran smiles, confused.

Fran Oh no that's, that's fine.

She sips from a glass of water. A pause. She is desperate to be asked a certain question.

83

I tried that thing you suggested by the way.

Lou What?

Fran He was quiet for like *a whole minute*.

Lou What did you do?

Fran I just said 'No'.
 I just said '*No I don't agree with that*' when he was
talking.
 And he was just –

She produces a stunned face.

It was amazing. I don't think a girl has ever said that to
him before –

Lou Sorry can we not talk about, Thingy actually
 Sorry. Just thinking about him makes me feel a bit
gross. He's just so – like in my worldview, like now –
awful.

Lou smiles, fake-gags, laughs.

Sorry. That's just how my brain is thinking about all of
That now.
 Lol.

A pause.

Fran No, no, that's, um. Fine. We can talk about
something else.

A pause.
 Tosh googles a word on her laptop. She smirks at it.
 Lou tries to look at the screen.
 Fran fidgets.

How are you, Tosh?

Tosh looks at her.

Tosh What?

84

Lights change.

　Fran goes.

　Tosh tries to move. She can't.

　She actually picks up Lou's head quite roughly to get out from under it.

　She gets herself up. Immediately falls down. Dead leg.

　She remains on the floor a moment. She pulls herself to seating. Pulls her legs up, places feet on the floor.

　A Boy enters the auditorium, holding flowers. He has no discernible personality. He watches her do this.

　She judders her legs back to life.

　She sees him.

　She judders her legs some more.

　She tries, with some difficulty, to stand up, looking at him, wary.

　She joins him off the stage, leaving Lou still lying on the floor.

　Lights change.

SCENE EIGHTEEN

The Boy and Tosh, somewhere else. Bathed in a striking, foreign light.

Tosh Sorry.

　Sorry.

　I'm just. Processing. That.

　Just replaying the spool of it over and over in my head so as to make sense of it or. Or own it or. Commit it to memory.

　I'm.

　She laughs a little.

Sorry, actually I can't quite get my head round that you said that. Could you say it again?

Seriously. Could you?

He smiles.
    He pauses for effect.

Boy You're so fit.

A pause.
    Lights change.
    He goes.

SCENE NINETEEN

*Lou and Tosh are both standing. Tosh is bright, she has
brought fresh flowers. Beautiful. Foolishly over the top.
    If possible, she is somehow more beautiful now.
    A slightly longer than comfortable pause.*

Tosh So yeah thank you for being so supportive about
the whole thing I just feel like I couldn't've been so like,
Open To This Period Of Change, within myself, had I not
known I had a safety net of support underneath me. I am
so grateful for that.

*Lou nods, offers a smile. She is being very polite. She
pronounces all her t's.*

Lou No, that's. Great.

A pause.

Tosh When I look back on myself I realised I *wanted* to
hate, I thought it was all their fault but it isn't it isn't *all*
of them it's only *some* of them but some of them are
completely deserving of love.
    And you opened me up to the potential of love, you
taught me that, you

Lou Yeah, okay.

A pause. Tosh sits. Lou doesn't.

Tosh And I was hoping I did that for you too

I have been talking about this with Joseph and I think it was a mutually beneficial –

Like we were very crucial on each other's journeys, from one point to another

The name Joseph causes a tiny synapse to shatter in Lou's skull.

Tosh waits for a response. Lou says nothing. Tosh considers standing. Doesn't.

I was thinking I might forgive myself.

A moment of just breath.

All that crime. All that bile.

Forgiveness.

I was thinking what would that look like.

A pause. Lou does not answer.
Tosh stands again.

Anyway I just came to say thank you.

And to tell you that I like him so much. I like, *like* him so much, like I really like his whole – I like him.

Like if you were worried.

Nothing.

But yeah. But mainly the thank you.

She laughs. A pause.

Are you seeing anyone?

A pause.

Lou Yes.

A pause.

Tosh Great.

A pause.

What number are we on now?

Lou winces.
Tosh immediately regrets her words.
The absence of a reply fills the room.

Can I use your toilet?

Lou Yep. It's. Where it is.

Tosh doesn't really know what to do with the flowers
so carries them out with her.

You know what's the most piss annoying thing of all.

Tosh comes back in immediately, awkward.

Tosh Yes. Tell me.

Lou reacts a little to this benevolent expression of
words. Then –

Lou If you had to y'know deliver your story, your life
story, right.
The time, that you spent with me, here, would be, like,
I dunno what the word is.

We wait for her to get the word.

Negligible.

A strange, blank pause.

Tosh If –

Lou A sort of dead space between all the Things That
Happened To You.
You won't celebrate this. You won't, like, pore over this
for reasons why you are.
That'll be Significant Relationship's that's His
This. This isn't the story this was just a given. This was
all a given.

Tosh looks at her, not really understanding.

Tosh Yeah. That's so annoying.

A pause.
  Tosh shifts a little.
  Tosh goes to speak, stops.
  Goes for –

I love you, by the way.

  Lou thinks for a moment.

Lou Yeah I don't see how that's relevant.

  Lights fall.
  Lou sort of flops, inelegantly, to the floor.
  She grieves. She makes her grieving sound.
  It takes as long as it takes for her to collect herself
  back in again.
  Lights change.
  Fran comes and pulls her up. Folds her onto the sofa.
  She clears away the plates and cups and bits.
  She sits on the sofa next to Lou.
  She sits next to her. She hands her tea.
  Lou can be as visibly unpinned as she just was on
  the floor, but now she is upright. And has tea.
  Lights to full.

SCENE TWENTY

Fran I'm fine, thanks, how are you?

Lou I'm fine thanks, how are you?

  Fran laughs.
  She stops.

Fran That's funny –

Lou You don't have to say it's funny you can just

Fran Ha-ha, sorry
  I always do that

89

Lou I know.

Fran (*cruel?*) I'm sorry you miss her

Lou Y'know in French 'miss' means missing from you
That's the literal translation
I 'miss' her
This (*Gestures to her body.*) misses, has a missing
Susie Dent put that on Twitter and I couldn't get out of
bed for a day
That's my only news

Fran What?

Lou I feel mad? I always thought when I finally went
mad I would feel calm and normal in chaos but I *feel* like
madness in a swathe of fucking

She accidentally gestures at Fran.

House Salad?

A brief pause.

I wanna like put my hands on the room and *shake* all the
skin flakes up

A brief pause.

Fran Ugh.
Sorry.

A brief pause.

I actually have some news

Lou Why do people always precede Stuff with 'I have to
warn you about incoming Stuff'
It makes me create like fourteen different possibilities
and they're frankly way more interesting than whatever it
is you're going to – see, mad

Lou titters to herself.

Fran I broke up with Tristan.

A pause.
Lou frowns. Not understanding.

My fiancé.

A brief pause.

Lou Well,
It was probably unsustainable.

Fran looks at Lou. Hurt.
She buries it down almost immediately –

Fran Well I feel really good about it? I'm excited actually?

Nothing.

Like I haven't been single in so long?
And I saw this film *How to Be Single* and like Rebel Wilson was so *funny.*

A weird pause.

And I've started reading actually?
And it's Amazing
Like, have you read *Normal People*?

A pause.
Lou looks at Fran.

Lou Yep

Fran Didn't you think it was Amazing?

Lou Yep

Fran Like I feel like I'm suddenly all using this whole part of my brain
And it's
It's so exciting
Am I –
Am I allowed to say that?

Lou nods, absently.

Good, cos,
　　Cos I did.

Lou thrusts her tea at Fran.

Lou Sorry I'm just gonna get some water

Lou leaves the room. She goes to the bathroom and drinks water from the tap.
　　Fran waits. She gets out her phone, checks it. Nothing. She panics, puts it away.
　　She sings, barely audibly, to herself, Little Mix's 'You're the man, but I got the, I got the, I got the power' whilst lightly beating her chest. Stops.
　　Lou comes back in and sits down, Fran starts –

Fran Like it's exciting all of a sudden
　　I get to *do* things now
　　Like you
　　And I wanted to ask you something

Lou makes a breathless sign of irritation.

Sorry, are you okay?

Lou does an 'OK' sign with her fingers.

Lou Crystal.

Fran laughs a very little. She stops.

Fran I actually wanted to ask you something

Lou ASK IT
　　Sorry

Lou buries her head.
　　A brief pause. Fear?

Fran I

Lou's up again –

Lou This is my first appointment in a week. I haven't really been entertaining.

I bought a COS-MO-POLITAN for fuck's sake
My brain is DEE-raining out
Maybe I should read NORMAL PEOPLE again
Maybe I should watch a ROMANTIC COMEDY for
the purpose of SELF-CARE and SELF-SOOTHING
    Which one do I watch?
    What's the Romantic Comedy for this?

She goes for her laptop, changes her mind –

Fran *Miss You Already* is good and quite like girl um

Lou makes a small hum of pain.

Can I move in now Thingy's [gone]?

Lou One day when I am older this will be funny. I will
properly understand the irony and find it actually funny.
And I will have such a good story to tell my – Oh No! –
anyone. I just need some time. I just need to put some
more time between it and me, between the Crap It and the
Great Me.
    Is that how you feel?
    Is that how the Typical Narrative feels?

Fran What's that?

Lou Ohhh A LOAD OF OLD SHIT PROBS

A pause.

Fran (*some fear*) Can I please move in here please?

A brief pause. Lou looks at Fran.

Lou (*brightening*) I mean Yeah.
    That would be so Fun.

Nodding.

Fran Like I thought we could be like wild crazy girls who
like fuck up our lives again
    And maybe do shared dinners?

And you could teach me everything
Cos um
I wasn't even aware that like I was um I was more
afraid of losing him than I liked him until you said it

Lou When did I say that

Fran Well you and Thingy used to always sort of –
I heard
I can hear

A brief pause.

(*Brave.*) I'm not stupid, by the way.

Lou looks at Fran.

You shouldn't be mean to me, Lou. I'm here.
I know I'm not [her], but
I'm not stupid I'm not
Stupid and I'm actually here –

Lou stares ahead.

Lou I wish I was stupid.

A pause.

Fran Do you ever think that maybe if she'd just kissed a
few more people we would never have had to worry
about this stuff?

Lou What?

Fran I dunno. I don't think I said that right.

A pause. Fran looks away from Lou.

But yeah it'll be soo fun.

A brief pause.
Lou is frowning.

Lou Was he always called Tristan?

94

*Fran looks at her, despairing. Lou tries out 'Tristan' in
her mouth.*
    *Fran suddenly starts to cry. She stops, almost
immediately.*

Fran (*self-chastising*) No.

A pause.
    Lou looks at Fran.
    She points very directly at Fran. Very strong.

Lou No. That's okay. You can do that here. You can do
that here.

Lights change.
    Tosh walks in.
    Lou stands up to meet her.
    Fran stays seated, staring.
    Lights to full.

SCENE TWENTY-ONE

Tosh is a little breathless.
    A pause.

Tosh I kept waiting for it.

A pause.
    Lou waits.

The big change that comes from uh Being Loved I
    I always thought there was a
    Um

A brief pause as Tosh searches.

Fran Sorry are you –

Tosh / No

Lou No

Fran covers her mouth, instinctively. She sits very still.
Lou and Tosh stare at each other.

Tosh The Big Change that comes from Being Loved?
I thought it was a glow
or
An underlining? Maybe?

A brief pause.

Didn't happen.

Lou You said.

Tosh I

She thinks about the right words for this.

I did a really good impression of Girlfriend.
I've seen enough of them.

A pause. They stare at each other, hard. Fran uncovers
her mouth and breathes very quickly and quietly.

But it's all right.
I came back.

A pause.

I mean he wasn't funny

They stare at each other.
Something passes between them.
It's done.
It takes every fibre of Lou's being to not run to Tosh.
After a moment, Tosh gently turns her head to
Fran.

(*True.*) I'm so sorry, hun.

A beat.
Fran understands.

Fran No it's. No it's [fine]

96

They wait.
Fran realises the implication.

I, uh

She gathers up her things in an ungainly way. Closes her laptop. Picks up her mug.
They wait.
This takes as long a time as it needs for her to take her small self out of their world.
She stands and makes to leave.
Tosh smiles at her, warmly.
She pauses by the door and looks back at them. She sort of nod-bows, and goes.
A pause.
Lou runs and grabs Tosh, almost winding her. It is necessary and hard, not euphoric. Tosh drops the flowers.
She holds and holds and holds.

Lou Oh my god. It's Tosh.

After some time, they separate.
They smile at each other.

SCENE TWENTY-TWO

Dido's 'White Flag' plays.
Tosh suddenly dips Lou, like an old Hollywood movie. They laugh.
Confetti rains down.
They come to standing.
Flowers grow throughout the room. Out of mugs. In between the cracks in sofa cushions. It is absurd and beautiful.
The lights grow, the space seems to grow, warmer, happier somehow.
Lou brings out a cheese sandwich.

They halve it and eat it on the sofa together.
Lights to full.
Lou laughs a little to herself. Tosh laughs a little to herself, unsure of what the joke is, perhaps a hangover from another joke. Happy.
Calm movement in silence.
Tosh goes into the bathroom to get some water.
When Tosh returns, Lou gets out her laptop.
Tosh does the same.
Tosh sits a little closer to Lou.
Lou changes position.
Tosh finishes her sandwich. She feels Lou looking at her.
A silence.
Tosh looks at Lou.
She hands Lou her crusts, Lou eats.
Tosh watches her for a while.
Lou feels aware of Tosh looking at her. After a while she smiles, self-consciously.
An answer to a question that hasn't been asked –

Tosh I'm not gonna leave you, by the way

   Beat.

Lou I know?

   A pause.
     Lou thinks about starting to say something.

[Did you think –]

   Tosh looks at her.

Tosh What?

   A brief pause.

Lou No, I. I wasn't gonna say anything.

   Lights fall.
     A bit of time in the dark.
   End.